Bless You —
Charles L. Allen

Perfect Peace

BY Charles L. Allen

God's Psychiatry
The Touch of the Master's Hand
All Things Are Possible Through Prayer
When You Lose a Loved One
The Twenty-Third Psalm
Healing Words
The Life of Christ
Prayer Changes Things
The Sermon on the Mount
Life More Abundant
The Charles L. Allen Treasury
When You Graduate (with Mouzon Biggs)
The Miracle of Love
The Miracle of Hope
The Miracle of the Holy Spirit
What I Have Lived By
Christmas (with Charles L. Wallis)
You Are Never Alone
In Quest of God's Power
Perfect Peace

Perfect Peace

Charles L. Allen

grason
1303 Hennepin Avenue
Minneapolis, Minnesota 55403

Scripture quotations in this volume are from the King James Version of the Bible, unless otherwise identified.

Scripture quotations identified RSV are from the Revised Standard Version of the Bible, copyrighted 1946, 1952, © 1971 and 1973.

Excerpt from "Sunrise at Campobello" by Dore Schary © Copyright 1958 by Dore Schary is used by permission of the publisher, Random House, Inc.

Excerpts from "Gambler" and "Faith" by G. A. Studdert-Kennedy are reprinted by permission of Hodder & Stoughton Limited.

"Stopping by Woods on a Snowy Evening" is from THE POETRY OF ROBERT FROST edited by Edward Connery Lathem. Copyright 1923, © 1969 by Holt, Rinehart and Winston. Copyright 1951 by Robert Frost. Reprinted by permission of Holt, Rinehart and Winston, Publishers.

Library of Congress Cataloging in Publication Data

Allen, Charles Livingstone, date
Perfect peace.

1. Consolation. 2. Peace of mind. I. Title.
BV4905.2.A39 248'.86 79-13040
ISBN 0-8007-1055-X

Published by Fleming H. Revell Company

Printed in the United States of America

TO

my wife,

Leila Haynes Allen,

who died September 24, 1978—

AND TO

our granddaughter,

Meredith Ann Allen,

who was being born in the same hospital

at the exact moment when her grandmother died

Preface

One does not have to live very long in order to find out that life can be hard and sometimes cruel—and sometimes almost impossible. Speaking to His disciples, and speaking also to every one of us, Jesus said, ". . . In the world ye shall have tribulation . . ." (John 16:33). He did not say that "maybe" ye shall have tribulation; He said, "Ye *shall* have tribulation." There is no *maybe* about it; it is as certain as life itself. One definition of tribulation is "a condition of affliction and distress."

There is a little verse that I have carried in my mind for many years. I have no idea where or when I first learned it, but defeat is speaking, and this is what defeat says:

> To him who tries and fails and quits—
> I am the foul blow.
> But, to him who in defeat,
> The lessons of life would learn—
> I lead through darkness and disaster
> To where the scarlet lights of triumph burn.

When defeats come, there are many responses we can make. In the following pages we shall look at some of the more common responses to defeat.

I especially appreciate Mrs. Constance Ward, my secretary, who helped me so very much in the preparation of this manuscript.

CHARLES L. ALLEN

Contents

1 Disappointment

Look first at disappointment. We dream and we hope and we set our hearts on certain goals. Then the time comes when we realize that our dreams are not coming true. This is an experience that happens eventually to every person. In this connection, I call to mind the greatest Christian preacher who ever lived—Saint Paul. Read carefully these words:

> After they were come to Mysia, they assayed to go into Bithynia: but the Spirit suffered them not. And they passing by Mysia came down to Troas.
>
> Acts 16:7, 8

That simply says that Paul's heart was set on going to Bithynia. If you are familiar with his life and the circumstances of this experience, you know this was his dream. This is what he wanted the most. Bithynia was the richest province in all of Asia, but somehow circumstances prevented him going there. Instead, he ended in Troas, a place he despised, had no interest in, and in which he could see no future.

This has happened to a lot of people. We set our minds and hearts on some Bithynia, and then we end up in some Troas.

The Troas in Some Famous Lives

One of the cities that I like to visit is Boston. In that delightful city, where there are so many historic sights to see, I have made my way at least half a dozen times to Old Trinity Church. There I stood on the sidewalk and looked at the statue of Phillips Brooks. There are very few ministers whose statues have been placed in front of churches they have formally served. In fact, this is the only one that comes to my mind at the moment. However, the dream of Phillips Brooks was to be a teacher, but as a teacher, he miserably failed. His Bithynia was denied him, but in his Troas he found immortality.

Every so often I read again the novel *The Citadel.* I really think it is my favorite of all the novels I know. It was written by A. J. Cronin, who was a medical doctor. His health failed and he was forced to give up his work. He ended up in a little town, despondent, defeated, and unhappy. He began to write, but he decided his writing was so poor that he took it and threw it in the garbage can. Later, he reluctantly retrieved the pages he had written and eventually they were published. His Bithynia was the practice of medicine, but had he stayed there, we would never have heard of him. His Troas was writing.

Read these words that Dr. Cronin wrote in *The Citadel:*

> Not far from his hotel, in a quiet side street [Manson] passed the open doorway of a church. Once again impulse caught him, caused him to stop, retrace his steps and enter. It was dark inside, empty and warm, as though a service had not long ended. He did not know what church it was, nor did he care. He simply sat down in the back seat of all and fixed his haggard gaze upon

> the dark enshrouded apse . . . He had never been a churchgoer, but now here he was, in this unknown church. Tribulation brought people here, brought people to their senses, brought people to the thought of God.

Whenever I read *The Citadel,* I am glad A. J. Cronin wrote his books.

One thinks of Sir Walter Scott, whose dream was to be a poet. That was his Bithynia. But if he had succeeded there, we would never have had such novels as *Waverley, Ivanhoe, Kenilworth, Old Mortality, Rob Roy, The Heart of Midlothian.* I am glad that he was disappointed as a poet, so that he was forced to write prose.

Here is another wonderful example. Listen to these words:

> . . . I am Joseph your brother, whom ye sold into Egypt. Now therefore be not grieved, nor angry with yourselves, that ye sold me hither: for God did send me before you to preserve life.
>
> Genesis 45:4, 5

We recall the background of those words. Joseph had gone to visit his brothers in the field. Being jealous of him, they had first put him into a deep hole in the ground; later they took him out of the ground and sold him to some Egyptians into slavery. Imagine this young boy growing up a slave. The important point is he did grow up, he did not quit, and he became a man of great power in that country. When his brothers came to buy grain for their starving people, he could see the providence of God in all that had happened.

Every so often, we need to say to ourselves, *My disappointment may be God's appointment.*

Go back to Paul. Out of his disappointment came the

establishment of the Christian faith in Europe, which eventually secured it. Had he gone to Bithynia, it is very possible we would never have heard of him or his faith again.

In His Heart

Whenever I think of disappointment, I always think of David. In my estimation, David was the greatest man who lived before Christ. There is no way that civilization can ever pay its debt to David. However, in the greatest dream of his life, he met bitter disappointment. He was successful as a musician, as a giant killer, as a general of the army, as a king, and as a literary genius. None of these things were what he wanted most. More than anything, he wanted to build the Temple. He had the plans drawn, he selected the site, and even purchased some of the materials, but he never accomplished his dream. He never saw the Temple. His son, Solomon, built it, but David was denied that privilege. David died a disappointed man. He felt that he had failed. In his own mind, and in the thinking of the world, he did fail to accomplish his greatest dream.

On an office wall I saw this slogan:

> *57 Rules for Success*
> FIRST, DELIVER THE GOODS.
> SECOND, THE OTHER 56 DO NOT MATTER.

According to that standard, David and many others have failed. But listen to these words: "And the Lord said unto David my father, Whereas it was in thine heart to build an house unto my name, thou didst well that it was in thine heart" (1 Kings 8:18). God reversed the judgment of David and the people of his world. In God's mind, David was a successful builder of the Temple. It was in his heart and

God gave him credit for the accomplishment. Many of our human judgments are reversed in the Heavenly Court. Many that we put first on this earth, God may put last. Many who look like failures here, in the bye and bye, may receive the applause and honor of eternity.

The Scottish writer, Ian Maclaren, wrote a beautiful story about a young man named Georgie Howe. Georgie went to the university to prepare for the ministry. He was a brilliant student and won highest honors. He was wonderfully prepared; but just after he received his diploma, instead of entering the ministry, he entered a sickroom. He longed to preach the Gospel, but he died without ever speaking one sermon.

The record of Georgie Howe in this world is blank. But in God's book, we have reason to believe that he is credited with tremendous victories that were in his heart.

Some of us feel embarrassed and disappointed at our accomplishments. We wish we might have done more, and we have a sense of frustration and failure. We need to remember that the final judgment is not our actual *accomplishments,* but rather, our *intentions*. There are more "successful failures" than we know about.

The Mystery of Pain

Again and again, we are compelled to admit that pain—hurt—suffering—is a mystery. Over and over we ask the question *Why did this happen?* only to be answered by a profound silence. Perhaps a clue to the answer is in the fact that so many of life's possibilities come in pairs—goodness and evil, short and tall, strong and weak, hot and cold—and also, pain and pleasure. The reality of one carries with it the possibility of the other. If we want success to be a possibility, then we must also accept defeat as another possibility.

It is easy to say, "What have I done to deserve this?" The answer may very well be "Nothing." On the other hand, look at so many of your blessings and ask that same question, and you get that same answer. Most of us have received far more and better things than we deserve. Write all of your disappointments on one page. Write all of your blessings on another page. Then ask yourself this question, "Would I be willing to give up my blessings in order to eliminate all of my disappointments?" When we really look at life, most of us would pretty much keep it as we have it.

Certainly we have had our disappointments. Our minds go back to the man in the Bible who was at the Pool of Bethesda. For thirty-eight years he had been there, hoping to get into the water at the right moment and be healed. It has been estimated that this paralyzed man could have made as many as fourteen thousand attempts during those thirty years. Think of being disappointed fourteen thousand times! Yet he stayed with it; he did not give up, and eventually those welcome words, "Rise, take up thy bed, and walk" (John 5:8).

2 Denial

"Wait Till Next Year"

Oftentimes, when an athletic team has been defeated, one hears the cry, "Wait till next year." This is one way of refusing to admit defeat. The truth is, no matter what happens next year, that team has been defeated this year. There are times when we need to accept defeat. Instead, many times we deny and reject the possibility of defeat. Nowhere do we see denial expressed more clearly than in the matter of death—the possibility of our own death, or the possibility of the death of a loved one. Often the response is that the doctor is mistaken; it just cannot be true; or, that some miracle will happen and everything will be changed. The truth is, many of us want to deny even the existence of death. In premarriage counseling, ever so often some couple will express objection to the words in the marriage ceremony "till death us do part." Many times the request has come to change that to such a phrase as, "as long as ye both shall live." They just do not want the word *death* spoken.

We hear people use the expression *passed away* or *expired,* but death is death, in spite of the fact that our reaction is to deny it. There was a dear grandmother who would never allow a certain drawer in her dresser to be opened. One day someone asked her what was in that drawer that was so sacred. She explained that she had carefully selected her burial clothes and put them in that drawer. She wanted to be sure that when that time came her body would be properly clothed before it was put in its final resting place. Most people would find it very depressing to select their burial clothes. They prefer to think there never will be a burial.

A prevalent attitude is to deny the existence of defeat, and death symbolizes the ultimate defeat.

At this point, we see a great difference between adults and children. Children experience loss in many ways. In our modern society, playmates move away; toys are broken; a loved dog gets run over by a car; a new baby is born into the home and someone else is getting more attention; and in many other ways the little child can feel the pangs of defeat.

When this happens they just act naturally; that is, they cry. They come running to Mama; they express their feelings in every possible way. Again and again, children feel helpless and hopeless; they do not try to explain it—they just feel it.

As we grow older, we are confronted with platitudes such as, "Be brave," or "You will get over it," or "You knew this had to come," and on and on.

One of the tragedies is that we as adults do not deal honestly with children in reference to defeat, and especially to death. We say, "Your father has gone on a long trip." That is not the truth and later on it is something that must be unlearned.

We say to a child, "Your mother (or your sister) is now living in heaven." However, that child saw that mother or sister being buried in the ground; thus a conflict is set up.

A child is told, "Your grandfather died because he was

sick.'' Later on when that child gets sick, he begins to worry because he associates sickness with death.

One of the worst things that we say to a child is ''God took your little brother because He needed someone good and sweet to live with Him in heaven.'' The child can very reasonably begin to wonder if being a good person is rewarded by death.

We can say to a child that someone ''has gone to sleep for a long time.'' Unless death and sleep are understood, that can develop in the child a fear even of going to bed at night.

The point is, let us be as honest as we can be as to what death really is. Let us give expression to our feelings. Why not cry? Tears are Godgiven in the right circumstances. Grief and sorrow needs to be recognized and expressed.

Death Is Not Defeat

As we study human beings, we must recognize that there are several essentials which we all must possess. The first one of these is *identity*. We want to be known; we want people to call our names; we like to see our names in print. One of our greatest fears is the fear of anonymity. When a person feels that he or she is a nobody—nobody knows him, nobody cares about him, nobody thinks of him—then defeat becomes very real for that person.

Another thing every person needs is *stimulation*. We want some excitement in living. Monotony is a deadening experience. We want to be made glad—to be made to feel alive. When life is dull and flat, it naturally breeds anxiety and leads to a deadening of the spirit, to a feeling of defeat. In this state, there is no goal and no purpose and no meaning in existence.

A third great need of every person is *security*. We are

disturbed by the news of the crime that is rampant in the cities in which we live. As we read the newspaper and listen to the news on radio and television, we wonder if there is any security at all. Our anxieties begin to grow. As we read of murders and suicides and accidents and deaths from every cause, we begin to wonder about our own death and what lies beyond. The question "What happens to us after we die?" becomes a frightening thought for most of us.

Let it be emphasized that *death is not defeat*. Instead, death is the greatest dimension of life. Death is the doorway to immortality. Death is the assurance that there is something within us that never dies.

There is a lovely story of an old man planting a tree. A young man said to him, "At your age, you will never see that tree grown up. Isn't it silly for you to spend your time and effort in planting it?" The old man replied, "When I was born in this world, there were trees that others had planted. I plant this tree so that when others are born, there will be trees for them to enjoy." Death is not defeat; death is immortality.

The Fatal Impression That Defeat Is Final

We have a dream which is not realized. We feel disappointment. We decide life is not worth living. One way or another we feel defeat. Let us overcome the fatal impression that defeat is final.

It has been said, "Opportunity knocks but once." That is simply not true; opportunity knocks many times. Often we need to remember that we are not defeated—our victory is just postponed. If life knocks us down, in the name of common sense, why cannot we get up again?

Here is a little poem that I have known for many years.

The words are wonderful, and it goes like this:

> They do me wrong who say I come no more
> When once I knock and fail to find you in;
> For every day I stand outside your door,
> And bid you wake, and rise to fight and win.
>
> Wail not for precious chances passed away,
> Wail not for golden ages on the wane!
> Each night I burn the records of that day;
> And at sunrise every soul is born again.
>
> WALTER MALONE "Opportunity"

Let's wrap this section up with a good story. There was a man by the name of Roswell McIntyre. He was a boy from a rural area in New York state, who was drafted into the Union Army in 1861. With very little training, he was sent into battle as a member of the cavalry. He had never experienced anything like war, and he became frightened and ran away. Eventually he was captured, tried, and sentenced to be shot as a deserter.

His dear mother went to Washington to see President Abraham Lincoln. He graciously granted an interview. As the tears rolled down her cheeks, she begged—as any mother would—for the life of her boy. The man representing the US Army replied, "Mr. President, we will destroy discipline in the army if we let this boy go. We must be firm."

After listening to both sides, Mr. Lincoln took a piece of paper and began to write on it. I have been told by a friend that that piece of paper today can be found framed, hanging on a wall in Washington. On the paper the President wrote, "If Roswell McIntyre will return to the Third New York Cavalry, and serve out his enlistment, or until otherwise discharged, he is hereby pardoned of any supposed desertion." I especially like that gentle gesture: *of any supposed desertion.*

Many people considered Roswell McIntyre a deserter and therefore a failure. Abraham Lincoln gave him another chance to prove that he could be a success. We do not need to face defeat as though it were permanent, because it need not be.

Draw a circle around these words: *Defeat must be faced, but it need not be final.*

3 Anger

Another reaction to defeat is anger.

Let's start with this question: Whoever promised you that you would live a life without hurts, disappointments, defeats, and all the other experiences that make us unhappy? Certainly you were never promised escape from death for yourself or one of your loved ones. Never having been promised immunity, then why do we get so angry when something happens?

Over and over, it has been said, "Why did this happen to me? I have lived a good life; I do not deserve this."

Before we become so bitter and angry, let us remind ourselves that we *do* live in a world of conflict. Yet we cry, "Why does God let this happen to me?"

The oldest book in the Bible is the Book of Job. This question of anger over seemingly undeserved experiences in life is the very center of that book. Look at Job's story. He was rich and successful. He owned seven thousand sheep, three thousand camels, five hundred yoke of oxen. He had great fields and servants by the hundreds to toil in those fields. He enjoyed a position of power and prestige, and he had a sense of security, but one day his "bank" failed—his "stock market" crashed. He became poverty-stricken. That is a hard blow.

Then a man came to his house and said to him, "All of

your children have been killed." They were visiting the house of their eldest brother and a cyclone came crashing in upon them. Job had a funeral for his seven sons and three daughters. It is hard to see how any human being could bear such an experience.

Then came the loss of his health. He was afflicted by painful boils. Every time he moved, it meant pain. He was ostracized from society, deserted by his friends, and forced to live in the city's garbage dump.

Now comes the turning point in Job's life. His wife is speaking, and we can identify with her words. Here is what she says, ". . . Dost thou still retain thine integrity? curse God, and die" (Job 2:9).

Curse God, and die. Job's wife is not the last person to utter that thought. Where is there one among us who has not felt the injustice of life to the point that we felt like saying in anger, "God, You are not fair." Most of us can remember at some point saying to our mothers or fathers, "I hate you." We felt that we were being mistreated and we gave vent to our anger. Anger is one of the normal emotions of mankind. In fact, anger can be good.

Before we condemn ourselves too harshly for some previous expression of anger, let us look more positively at this emotion.

There is a story of a university president who, among other duties, had the responsibility of raising money to support the university. He was a delightful personality, with the charm and the ability to make friends and influence people. One of his faculty members was constantly getting into the news with statements that disturbed possible donors to the university. One day the president was scheduled to speak in chapel and he especially invited this young professor to attend. That day he spoke in his charming manner, emphasizing the great tact and diplomacy of Jesus. He explained carefully how through the use of simple stories and loving words, Jesus persuaded people. He explained how that when Jesus spoke, ". . . the common people heard him gladly" (Mark 12:37).

After the chapel service, as they left together, the young professor said, "I now better understand what you mean. I shall try to follow the principles so beautifully pointed out in your address today." Naturally the president was very happy and felt that he had won his victory. But then the young professor said, "There is one thing, however, that bothers me. If Jesus was so beautifully tactful and diplomatic, how did He manage to get Himself crucified?"

The truth is, Jesus did not always accept life as He found it. There are times when He rebelled against the circumstances of His day and of His own life. There were times when He angrily denounced certain people as "vipers" and "hypocrites" (Matthew 3:7; Matthew 16:3). We need to outgrow the immature idea that anger is always sinful. The truth is, no emotion is sinful, but every emotion can be used in a sinful way. Anger can be a powerful energy of the soul. But it can also be a destructive force in a human life.

Is Not Power

On the negative side of our anger, let us remember first, that anger is not power. Anger can very definitely be loss of control. It's a wonderful thing to be able to drive your car down the highway, but if your car goes out of control, then it becomes an instrument of death. Much of our anger is weakness and not strength. It is emotional immaturity; it is arrested development. Anger in a child is a normal response, but as we grow we should, in the words of Paul,

". . . put away childish things" (1 Corinthians 13:11). Really, uncontrolled anger is childish and unbecoming to a mature person.

Is Selfish

In the second place, much of our anger is a very unbecoming expression of selfishness. We are thinking about how we have been hurt, or somebody got what we wanted. When it is all over, we are the ones who are hurt.

It has been said that the deafness of the great musician Beethoven was caused by a sudden fit of anger. If that is true, think of the tragedy here. The great musician could never hear even his own music.

Sometimes people say, "I get angry quickly, but I get over it." You can say the same thing about a cyclone. It doesn't linger around very long, but it does a lot of damage while it's there.

There are many times in every life when we need to remember the familiar words, "He that is slow to anger is better than the mighty; and he that ruleth his spirit than he that taketh a city" (Proverbs 16:32).

Can Be Misdirected

Another thing we need to remember is that, though anger is good, it can be misdirected. We can get angry at the wrong things and the wrong people.

We do not ask God to take away our temper, our anger, or to even lessen our ability to experience that emotion or that protest. We do not want to become less a person than we really are. We *do* ask God to give us control and judgment.

We would not condemn those hearty Bostonians who

threw the tea in the sea and who said, ''We will be subject to a foreign nation no longer.'' We do not condemn those people who said that filthy, disease-ridden prisons should be tolerated no longer. We do not condemn those who said that racial intolerance has become intolerable in our nation. In fact, anger is often an expression of love. We cannot indifferently stand by while people are being hurt by wrongs in our society. If we love enough, we will get angry over the things that hurt them. Moses felt anger toward Pharaoh. Lincoln felt angry toward slavery. Many of the wrongs in our society exist because they are tolerated.

Here is a good place to insert the wise words of Aristotle. He said, ''Anybody can become angry—that is easy, but to be angry with the right person, and to the right degree, and at the right time, and for the right purpose, and in the right way—that is not within everybody's power and it is not easy.''

Here I would also like to quote the words of another wise person. Plutarch put it this way, ''I have learned that anger is not incurable, if one wants to cure it.''

Not the Anger of God

When defeat comes—in whatever form—above all things, let us not feel that it is because of the anger of God. Over and over, across the years, brokenhearted people have expressed the thought that this would never have happened, if God had not been angry with them. If I believe for one moment that God would let my child or my wife die because He was angry for something I had done, I would despise that God with all my being. Such a God would not be worthy of being God. We need to know that there is nothing you can do to make God love you more than He does love you. There is also nothing you can do to make God hate you as a person. God may hate our sins, but He loves every one of His children.

As the years go by, our language changes. I rarely hear anybody talking today about the "grace" of God. We sing the hymn "Amazing Grace," but really, that word *grace* is not part of our daily language.

Speaking of changes in language, last Christmas I heard a teenager singing a song and the words sounded strange to me. I asked her to sing it slower so I could get the words, and this is what she sang: "Jingle bells, shotgun shells—rabbits all the way. O what fun it is to ride in a souped-up Chevrolet." That isn't the way *I* learned that song, but it sounded pretty good as she sang it!

Anyway, we have heard quoted time and time again the words of John Newton. Standing on a street one rainy day, he saw a man being led in chains to the jailhouse. As he stood there and looked at that man, tears ran down his face, and he said, "But, for the grace of God—there goes John Newton." God is not angry with us; God's grace is sufficient for all our needs.

The wrong anger is not the right response to a seeming defeat.

4 Fear

We make various responses to seeming defeat. I say *seeming* because I do not believe that defeat is ever final. It is a momentary situation and there is always another chapter to be written. One of the responses we make to it at the moment is fear. Our seeming defeat may come in many forms. There is sickness, the death of a loved one, the loss of a job, bankruptcy, and an endless number of other ways.

It is a strange coincidence that the Bible repeats the command "Fear not" exactly 365 times—or once for each day of the year. It is as if to say there is no day in our lives when fear is not a present reality. There is a tendency to deny the presence of fear. On the other hand, when one recognizes the presence of faith, there is no longer need to deny fear. Once you emphasize your faith, you are not hesitant to recognize and cope with your fears. When we have faith, we can assure ourselves that it is perfectly all right to be afraid. Being fearful is not unchristian and neither is it weakness. Recognizing fear is a sign not only of faith, but of courage and confidence. One has come a long way in life when one reaches the point at which he or she cares to face fear.

Handling Fear

Let me say three things about fear.

(1) *Admit it.* Maybe you do not need to shout it from the housetops, but at least in your own heart face up to the fact that you are afraid. The very recognition of fear is a victory within itself. It is a strong step toward self-confidence. Many times we feel afraid when we are alone, or feel abandoned, or rejected, or misunderstood, or isolated, or uncertain. We feel that no one can handle it for us, and we do not have the confidence to believe we can handle it alone.

(2) *Accept it.* If one is sick, and lurking in the darkness is the fear of "sickness unto death," one can say that the doctor has made a mistake, that it cannot be true. The same may be said of any of our fears. But some things are true, and some things are not going to be changed, and some things must be lived with. When we *accept* fear, then we are ready for the third step.

(3) *Deal with it.* Acceptance is never easy and it may be painful. But it is also freeing. We reach the point that we do not have to pretend any more, not even to ourselves. We do not have to feel that we are failures, or that we are weak, or that we are different from other people. We can escape that feeling that somehow we are guilty, and we can stop running and trying to hide.

Instead, we can stop and hurt, if we want to.

Identify Your Fear

To identify your fear is the first step in dealing with it. Let us remember that all the fears that any person has have been learned, they are not natural with the exception of just two. Many people feel that the two natural, unlearned fears are the fear of falling and the fear of a sudden loud noise.

Every other fear is one that we have picked up somewhere along the way of life. Here let me list some of the fears that are rather normal in people. To this list, add the ones that come to your mind—being alone; riding in an airplane; facing old age, being in the presence of death; losing your material possessions; your house being burned up; getting stuck on an elevator; the sight of blood; going to the dentist; losing your mind; talking to the boss; cancer; a heart attack; the end of the world—and to these fears every person can add many others.

Instead of worrying about how to get rid of all your fears, emphasize your faith to the point that you are willing to accept your fears and live with them. In fact, we can go even further and make friends with our fears. To begin with, we recognize the fact that fear is constructive and positive and important in every human life. Fear is not an enemy and we need not worry about how to get rid of our fears. The truth is, fear is a God-given emotion for our protection and for our own good. There are many things that we should fear. I have heard it said, "If you don't draw us by love, you can never drive us by fear." That is not the truth. We obey the speed limit; we pay our income taxes; we visit the doctor; we do many things because we are afraid not to do them. Fear causes us to seek further knowledge. If man did not fear cancer, then all of the research carried on in the name of cancer would be stopped. The Bible tells us, "The fear of the Lord is the beginning of wisdom . . ." (Psalms 111:10). Once we recognize the fear, then we seek to learn how to cope with it.

Without fear there would be no faith. Fear is a stimulation to the very highest living.

Fear Is Not Failure

Let us be very clear at this point—*fear is not failure—fear is not weakness—fear need not be destructive—we do not need be ashamed of our fears—fear stimulates faith—fear is the inspiration to endeavor—fear is the doorway to wisdom*. Therefore, we do not need to fear fear.

I like the words of Joanna Baillie:

> The brave man is not he who feels no fear,
> For that were stupid and irrational;
> But he, whose noble soul its fears subdues
> And bravely dares the danger nature shrinks from.
>
> *Basil*

There are two things which we should not fear. One of them is that which we can change. If we can do something about it, let us stop wringing our hands in useless fear. Let's get to work to do something. The second thing we should not fear is that which we cannot change. If there is nothing we can do about it, then, to put it simply, there is nothing we can do about it.

One of the most prayed prayers in all the world is the prayer that Professor Reinhold Niebuhr wrote many years ago:

> God grant me the serenity
> To accept the things I cannot change;
> The courage to change the things I can,
> And the wisdom to know the difference.

Here is a good place to summarize some very fundamental principles in reference to fear. First, live one day at a time. You can't relive the past and you can't live the future.

There is no need to hold on to the failures of yesterday and to manufacture fears for tomorrow. Do the best you can now in spite of what has happened. I know this has been said over and over again, but I also know that we need to keep saying it.

Sir William Osler was a distinguished physician and teacher at Johns Hopkins and the University of Pennsylvania. This is what he said:

> The load of tomorrow, added to that of yesterday, carried today, makes the strongest falter.

He went on to say, "we should live in date-tight compartments, not letting yesterday and tomorrow intrude on our lives." He concluded, "Then, you will avoid the waste of energy, the mental distress, the nervous worries that dog the steps of the man who is anxious about the future."

Or as Balzac, the nineteenth-century French author, put it: "After all, our worst misfortunes never happen and most miseries lie in anticipation."

Do Something for Somebody

Another thing that needs to be said about fear is, it can be dealt with if we stop thinking about ourselves and start doing something for somebody else. If you feel a fear coming on, think of somebody who is lonely, or worried, or who needs help. Go down to the store and buy a present, and take it or send to that person. It is marvelous what that simple little act will do for you. Buying the present for somebody else oftentimes can do as much for you as a visit to a psychiatrist, and it is a lot less expensive.

Edward Everett Hale said something worth repeating:

To look up and not down,
To look forward and not back,
To look out and not in, and
To lend a hand.

I especially emphasize that last phrase "and to lend a hand."

George Bernard Shaw describes a certain person as "a selfish little clod of ailments and grievances, complaining that the world will not devote itself to making [him] happy." Unselfish service to others can turn even the utmost tragedy into victory. Let us remember well this truth—happy people are helpful people.

Trust in God

Then in the third place, when fear is before us, let us trust in God. This does not mean that God promises us escape from all the troubles of life, but we do have the promise of His fellowship and companionship. I am not a fatalist, but I believe that nothing will ever happen that God does not permit to happen.

One of the great psychologists was Jung. I remember that once he said, "The greatest and most important problems of life can never be solved, but only outgrown." Once I saw a little poster in the lobby of a hospital that read: "Worrying is like a rocking chair. It will give you something to do, but will get you nowhere." That is not true with fear. Fear will accomplish things. Fear is one of life's driving forces to help mankind reach the highest heights.

I think Van Dyke says it best in "The Voyagers"—

O Maker of the Mighty Deep,
Whereon our vessels fare,

Above our life's adventure keep
  Thy faithful watch and care.
In Thee we trust, whate'er befall;
The sea is great, our boats are small.

We know not where the secret tides
  Will help us or delay,
Nor where the lurking tempest hides
  Nor where the fogs are gray.
We trust in Thee, whate'er befall;
The sea is great, our boats are small."

We can deal with defeat without getting desperate, even though our boats are small, when we recognize that defeat is not final. There was a time when Demosthenes, the great Greek orator, could no longer hide from the people the fact that he stuttered. Finally, he took it into the world, where people could see it, and he could begin to conquer his stuttering tongue. Steinmetz, the great scientist, came to believe that he could be a useful person in spite of the fact that his body was terribly deformed. Milton was blind, but eventually he believed that, in spite of his blindness, he could write poetry that could make life sing. Robert Louis Stevenson was sick. He suffered physical pain all of the time, but during his sickest years, he wrote some of his greatest masterpieces. Beethoven reached the point at which he believed he could give to the world a composition like the Ninth Symphony, even though he was deaf and could not hear it himself. Louis Pasteur made his greatest contribution after he had a stroke. We do react to certain situations with fear, but we also use fear as a springboard.

5 Memory—Guilt—Forgiveness

One of the most common reactions to the hard experiences of life is a feeling of guilt. Memory is a very blessed and wonderful ability of man, but memory can also make us very unhappy and depressed. When life is dark, there is a tendency to look back with deep regret, as we remember certain things we did and said.

Failure brings out remorse. If we were successful all the time, we would not have nearly as many regrets. It is after we have been defeated that we begin to look back with regret. For example, when a married couple is living happily together and everything is going well, they are not likely to remember their unhappy experiences. When one of them dies, however, there is a tendency to remember words and deeds that we wish had not been spoken and done; and also, to remember the things we might have said and might have done, but failed to do.

On the back page of an issue of *Creative Help for Daily Living,* published by Foundation for Christian Living, Pawling, New York, is this poem which sums up the feelings that, sometime or other, nearly all of us have.

Letter to Dad

There are so many things I'd like
To tell you face to face;

I either lack the words or fail
To find the time or place.
But in this special letter, Dad,
You'll find, at least in part,
The feelings that the passing years
Have left within my heart.

The memories of childhood days
And all that you have done
To make our home a happy place
And growing up such fun.
I still recall the walks we took,
The games we often played;
Those confidential chats we had
While resting in the shade.

This letter comes to thank you, Dad,
For needed words of praise;
The counsel and the guidance, too,
That shaped my grown-up days.
No words of mine can tell you, Dad
The things I really feel;
But you must know my love for you
Is lasting, warm, and real.

You made my world a better place
And through the coming years,
I'll keep these memories of you
As cherished souvenirs!

AUTHOR UNKNOWN

During times of strain and stress we are much more likely to remember things that bring us guilt, and one result of guilt is paralysis. Just as a car can become so mired in the mud, until it is stuck and can go neither forward nor backward, so can a person become mired in past mistakes and failures and become stuck and emotionally immobile.

One of the best illustrations of this fact comes out of the experience of Christ. He was visiting in a home in Capernaum (Mark 2:1–12). Such a crowd gathered that there was not room for anyone else to get into the house. There came four men bringing a man who was stricken with paralysis. They got on top of the house, cut a hole through the roof, and let the man down into the room where Jesus was. Jesus looked at that man, but He did not say, "Thy paralysis be healed." Instead He said, "Thy sins be forgiven thee." Then He said to the paralytic, "Arise, and take up thy bed, and go thy way . . . ." (v. 11).

The trouble with this man was not that he was paralyzed; his problem was a sense of guilt, and often it happens that, at the time when we most need our strengths and abilities, we are the most helpless and paralyzed. The reason is that we look back with sorrow and condemnation and guilt.

Guilt Is Not Always Bad

Let me hasten to say that guilt is not always a bad thing. The truth is, it is good if it has the right results. One difference between a sheep and a hog is, that when a sheep falls into a mudhole, it is uncomfortable and struggles to get out. When a hog falls into a mudhole, he wallows in it and enjoys it!

In his poem "Song of Myself," Walt Whitman says this:

> I think I could turn and live with animals, they are
> so placid and self-contained . . . .
> They do not lie awake in the dark and weep for their
> sins . . . .

But while animals do not weep for their sins, neither do they write poetry. A feeling of guilt can be a very human quality. But it can also be a very paralyzing experience. Across the years, I have had numerous experiences with people who are paralyzed by guilt. I tell you now about a man who was in such a nervous state he could not do his work. His business was about to fail; his homelife was rapidly deteriorating; he was avoiding his friends; he was getting himself into a terrible situation. He came to talk to me about something he had done, which he felt was extremely bad. He was haunted by it day and night. This was the reason for the collapse he was experiencing in his life.

He was deeply repentant, and he prayed constantly for forgiveness, but somehow the peace that he sought never came. I explained to him carefully about the forgiveness of God. It seemed to me that he met every condition to enable him to claim that forgiveness. But somehow, the peace just would not come. Finally I said to him, "God has done something for you that you are not willing to do for yourself. God has forgiven you but you have not forgiven yourself."

Then I told him to come with me and I led him to the altar of the church. I had him kneel and I explained to him that I was an ordained minister. I put my hands upon his head and I said, "In the name of Jesus Christ, who alone can forgive sins, I now declare that by His power you are forgiven. Your sins are taken away, and from this moment you are a free person."

Then I took him by the hand and told him to stand up. He stood on his feet and there suddenly came over his face a different look. He said with almost the tone of a shout, "It is gone! It is gone!"

God Paints in Many Colors

From that time on, this man's life has been completely different. Finally he believed in forgiveness and he accepted it. G. K. Chesterton says: "God paints in many colors, but He never paints so gorgeously as when He paints in white." As we think of various colors, we think of the crimson of the sunset, the blue of the ocean, the green of the trees in the springtime, the purple of a lovely flower, but, there comes a time when white is the most beautiful of all the colors God paints.

The prophet Isaiah said to the people, ". . . though your sins be as scarlet, they shall be as white as snow . . ." (Isaiah 1:18). There is no more precious or beautiful promise in the entire word of God. Forgiveness is a reality.

I have in my notes some words of Reinhold Niebuhr. Here is what he said:

> Nothing that is worth doing is completed in our lifetime; therefore, we must be saved by hope. Nothing true or beautiful or good makes complete sense in any immediate context of history; therefore, we must be saved by faith. Nothing we do, however virtuous, can be done alone; therefore, we are saved by love. No virtuous act is quite as virtuous from the standpoint of our friend or foe as from our standpoint. Therefore, we must be saved by that final form of love which is forgiveness.
>
> *The Irony of American History*

The good news of God is that He understands our humanness; He *forgives us;* He *accepts us;* He *loves us.*

Suppose You Had No Memory

Let us not condemn ourselves because of the memory of something past. Suppose you had no memory? Remembrance of the past preserves our identity. Without that memory we would never know who we are. We know that we are persons who are living now, but we must have in our minds the past in order to know what the now means. Forgetting the past results in an emptiness and a real lack of life today.

I heard of a person who said that he was tired of going to church and constantly hearing about the people in the olden days of the Bible. He said "I want to go to 'the church of what's happening now.' " That sounds good, but it is not good. The church that is not rooted and grounded in the past is not going to be effective in the now.

As we think of our past mistakes, let us also remind ourselves that our strengths and our abilities and our future is rooted and grounded in our past.

I read about a man who had a calendar on his wall which had only one day for each page. At the close of each day he would tear off that page and throw it in the wastebasket. To his consternation he realized that his calendar was growing thinner with each passing day. So, he changed his practice and instead of throwing the page for each day into the wastebasket, he carefully filed it with its predecessors. Then as the calendar grew thinner, the file of days he had lived grew thicker. So it is with life. Yes, we can look back with regrets and with guilts, but if you merely throw away the past, life for you gets thinner and thinner.

A minister friend of mine offered comfort to a mother whose child had recently died. This is what he said, "As burdensome as the grief of loss most certainly is, there is yet one grief heavier to be born than grief of loss, and that's the grief of never having possessed."

So we have possessed some past days and some past years. Maybe we did make some mistakes, though we also won some victories. We ask forgiveness for the mistakes and we are thankful for the good things. Because of the gift of memory, we are not impoverished because of what we have lost.

We have never lost it.

6 Is God Fair?

A controversial hymn in the official *Book of Worship,* used by the United States Forces, will be replaced by another hymn. The hymn being replaced is entitled "It Was on a Friday Morning" and the lyrics read:

It was on a Friday morning
That they took me from the cell,
And I saw they had a carpenter
To crucify as well.
You can blame it onto Pilate,
You can blame it on the Jews,
You can blame it on the Devil,
It's God I accuse.

Refrain:

It's God they ought to crucify
Instead of you and me,
I said to the carpenter
Ahanging on the tree.

Now Barabbas was a killer
And they let Barabbas go,
But you are being crucified
For nothing here below.
But God is up in heaven
And he doesn't do a thing:

With a million angels watching
And they never move a wing.

Repeat Refrain

To hell with Jehovah,
To the carpenter I said,
I wish that a carpenter
Had made the world instead.
Good-by and good luck to you,
The road will soon divide.
Remember me in heaven,
The man you hung beside.

Repeat Refrain

Many people could sing that song with feeling. God is accused again and again. The psalmist said, ". . . the judgments of the Lord are true and righteous altogether" (Psalms 19:9). Many people do not believe that is true. What about babies who are born with physical deformities? What about two mothers who prayed for their sons and one son is killed in an automobile wreck, while the other son gets along fine? How does the wife feel whose husband was forty years of age and died of a sudden heart attack—especially when she knows many other men who are that age still alive, although they are not living nearly as good lives as her husband did? When we come to the actual time of dealing with defeat, one of the reactions we can have is that God is not fair. That God has not treated us right.

Man's Free Will

In answer to this question we need to keep four facts in mind—first, in the very first chapter of the Bible we read of the creation of this world and how that God put man on earth, a free-will creature. Man chose to disobey God. Many of the things that we blame on God really should be blamed on man's disobedience.

I often think of the story of the little boy who pushed his little playmate into a ditch, hit him with a rock, and spat in his face. In scolding him, his mother said that he should have not let Satan cause him to treat his friend that way. The little boy replied, "Mother, Satan did tell me to push him in the ditch and hit him with the rock, but spitting in his face was my own idea."

Many of the evils of this world come as a result of man's rebellion against God.

Every so often, someone says to me, "I have lost faith in God." My reply is that the more important question we need to consider is, "Have we lived in such a way that God may have lost faith in us?"

More Rewards Than Defeats

This is part of the answer but it is not the entire answer. Second, we need to remember that there are more compensations and rewards in living than there are punishments and defeats. It is true that some things happen that seem unfair. On the other hand, we receive many blessings that we do not deserve. When trouble and hurt and disappointment and pain and defeat come into our lives we ask the question *"Why?"* But, we need to remember that justice triumphs much more often than we give it credit for. The psalmist declared "I believe I shall see the goodness of the

Lord in the land of the living'' (*see* Psalms 27:13). For the psalmist the ''land of the living'' is in this life. On the other hand, we cannot entirely judge by this life. Often we need to remind ourselves of these words, ''Reserve your judgment; time will vindicate God. If this life does not set you to singing again, then eternity will.''

God's Tender Mercy

In the third place, let us not forget God's tender mercy. Put two sheets of paper before you. On one sheet write everything you have done which was perfectly good with no touch of evil in it. On the other sheet put down everything you can remember that you have done that was wrong in any way. As you study your own list, you are likely to fall on your knees praying, ''God, be merciful to me, a sinner.'' There have been hurts and seeming injustices, but God has also been merciful and good.

Remember God's Own Son

Fourth, as we decide the fairness of God, let us consider the fact that God's own Son, Jesus Christ, was crucified at the age of thirty-three. It seemed to be a black and a terrible thing to happen, but now we refer to that day as ''Good Friday.'' Today, more people look to Him as their spiritual leader and their Saviour than have ever looked to any other person who ever lived on this earth. The Cross of Christ will forever stand as our supreme evidence of a loving, suffering, forgiving God.

One of the greatest Bible preachers and teachers who ever lived on this earth was William Barclay. A few days before she was to be married, his only daughter was drowned. Later in speaking about it, Dr. Barclay said this: "I am not so concerned as to whether or not Jesus stilled the tempest on the sea. What I do know is He stilled the tempest in my heart."

He did not attempt to explain the drowning of his daughter. He does testify to the healing mercy of God in that experience.

What Kind of a God?

Most people say, "I believe in God." But this is not enough. The question is, "What kind of a God do I believe in?"

I often recall the young man who went to his minister, proclaiming the fact that he did not believe in any god. The minister did not condemn him nor did he argue with him. He simply said, "Describe for me the god you do not believe in." The minister listened carefully, as the boy described the god he did not believe in. When he had finished, the minister replied, "Neither do I believe in that god. Now let's talk together about a God that we can believe in."

In the great chapter on love, 1 Corinthians 13, Paul declares, "[Love] is patient." Another way to say that is "Love can wait." The truth is many times it is compelled to wait. It is not easy, in the midst of defeat, to "wait and see." But many have found—even most of us—that "to wait is to see." Many of us have spoken the expression "Have patience with the patience of God."

Sometimes *to wait is to see* means waiting a year or ten years, or maybe into eternity. Because as Paul stated in the same chapter in which he wrote "[Love] suffereth long," he also declared, "Now we see through a glass, darkly; but then face to face . . ." (1 Corinthians 13:4, 12).

What we must simply say is that many things happen that we cannot explain.

Often we are told that we cannot bargain with God. We remind ourselves that God's favor cannot be bought. We reaffirm the fact that no matter what we do, God is still the same God. Over and over, I have reaffirmed these principles, but then sometimes I am not entirely sure. I am thinking now of a man who called his minister from a hospital about three o'clock one morning. His six-year-old son was in that hospital, and the doctors could not give the man any hope at all that the little boy would live. The man asked his minister if he would come and pray that his little boy would be spared.

When the minister got there the father told him about the way he had lived, leaving God out of his life. He told him how once he was faithful to God and had asked God to bless him in his business. He became almost instantly a success. It has been often said that it is hard to hold a full cup with a steady hand—especially when the cup is suddenly filled. This man had taught a Sunday-school class, he had faithfully attended church, and he had had prayer in his home, but now he was rich and successful and he didn't feel the need of God.

In talking to his minister, he said, "If God will let my little boy live, I will be faithful again in my life." Together they prayed, and the man sobbed out his vow of faithfulness.

The little boy did get well. Maybe he would have gotten well anyway. On the other hand, it just may be that because of this man's prayer that God did intervene. In my own faith, I find it hard to believe that I can bargain with God. On the other hand, I am not sure and if the truth is known, probably most of us—at some time or other—have sought to bargain with God. It just may be that God does hear and God does respond. I will say for myself: in time of great need, I am not above confessing to God, seeking His forgiveness and His guiding hand in the future. It is just possible that in certain moments one becomes a person into whose heart God can come.

7 We Can Possess Peace

One of the most poignant stories in all of literature is the one about David's son who was sick. It is found in chapter 12 of Second Samuel, beginning with the fifteenth verse. The son that his wife, Uriah, bore him was stricken. David began to pray that the child be saved. He fasted, he even, as the story says, "Lay all night upon the earth" (v. 16).

Friends and servants went out to him to get him to get up from the earth and come into the house. He would not get up; also he would eat nothing. This went on for seven days and then the child died. His servants were afraid to tell David that the child was dead, because they were afraid of what he might do to himself when he heard the news. David realized that the servants whispered and he knew in his heart that the child had died. Thus, David asked the servants, "Is the child dead?" They replied, "He is dead."

Then we read how David rose up from the ground, went in and took a bath, changed his clothes and went to the church and worshiped. Then, when he came home, he sat down at the table to eat.

The servants were really surprised at his actions. They reminded him how that he fasted and wept for the child while it was alive, but now that the child was dead, he ceased weeping and would eat.

David explained, "While the child was yet alive, I fasted

and wept: for I said, Who can tell whether God will be gracious to me, that the child may live? But now he is dead, wherefore should I fast? can I bring him back again? I shall go to him, but he shall not return to me'' (2 Samuel 12:22, 23).

When to Accept

Here is a marvelous example for every one of us who has had a crisis and especially a death in his family. It is even a marvelous example for facing his or her own death. As long as there was life, David did everything he possibly could. When death came, instead of ''cursing God,'' instead of ''drowning himself in sorrow,'' instead of saying *''Why—why—why?''* he accepted the fact that nothing could be done. He had done his best; now it was time to look to the future and go on. So, he could bathe, eat his dinner, and begin to think about tomorrow.

There is marvelous power and peace in acceptance. David accepted death without desperation.

Once on a vacation trip, my wife and I were driving through a desert in the western part of the United States. It was my habit to carry my money in a clip in my pants pocket. For some reason, I felt in that pocket and my money was gone. I stopped the car, we got out and searched thoroughly behind the seat and throughout the car. I felt in all of my pockets. I even opened my suitcase and went through that, and I looked in the pockets of clothes I had worn the day before, but the money was not to be found. I sat there bemoaning our loss and then my wife said, ''Are we just going to sit here in the desert worrying about what we have lost, or are we going to go on?'' So, I started the car and we continued the trip. We were able to work things out and had a good trip.

Since that experience, there have been several occasions when life did not go for me as I had planned. When I had a problem to worry about, the thought would come to me, "Am I going to just sit here in the desert worrying, or am I going to go on?" There are some times in every life when we need to stop worrying and start going again. We accept what has happened, but we realize it is not the end of our world.

I had the high privilege of once visiting with Pope Paul VI. He is the only pope with whom I ever had any personal contact, thus when he died, it had special meaning for me. I read with interest all the accounts of his funeral. When he was buried, there began a specific period of mourning, which came to an end after a specified number of days. Then the Cardinals began their meeting to elect a new pope.

The many, many people who loved Pope Paul VI will continue to hold him in their hearts, but they will also accept the new pope and the church will continue its work.

So it is in life, we accept and then we keep going. Acceptance and peace go together. One leads to the other.

One of the Bible verses which is a favorite of many of us is Isaiah 26:3: "Thou wilt keep him in perfect peace, whose mind is stayed on thee: because he trusteth in thee." There is a beautiful melody and great inspiration in those words: *perfect peace*.

Empty Our Minds

This verse brings to mind two actions we need to take. First, we need to empty our minds. I live in a house which has a large attic. It is so convenient to put things in the attic, and across the years there had accumulated a vast number of articles—some of them worthless and useless. I keep telling myself that I need to clean out my attic and give to some charitable organization all those articles that I cannot use. But somehow I keep putting it off. I suspect that there are many attics that need to be cleaned out.

When I come home at night one of the first things I do is wash my hands, sending down the drain the dirt that has accumulated.

Wouldn't it be a wonderful thing if we could clean out our minds as we can clean out our attics? or wash out our minds as we can wash our hands?

After Rabbi Joshua Liebman wrote his book *Peace of Mind,* he was swamped with people seeking that peace. His mail was heavy; his telephone rang constantly; many people came to see him. He was a young, kindhearted rabbi, only thirty-eight years old. He tried to help every person and he died in just three years at the age of forty-one. He just could not stand up to the burden. But before he died, he said, "I am appalled at the multitude of people who have never learned to empty their minds."

There are two types of unfamiliar hymns. One is the hymn that we have never heard or sung before. However, another hymn that is unfamiliar is the one we have sung so many times that we sing it and never think about it. The words literally become meaningless. Many of us have sung "What a Friend We Have in Jesus" since we were children. We sing it without thinking. If we would sing it *with* thinking, it could literally change our lives. Here let me quote the words of the first verse. Let us read it and think about what it says as we read:

> What a friend we have in Jesus,
> All our sins and griefs to bear!

What a privilege to carry
Everything to God in prayer!
O what peace we often forfeit,
O what needless pain we bear,
All because we do not carry
Everything to God in prayer!

As we look back over our lives, we can remember hurts, losses, mistakes, wrongs, and other deeds that we have done. We also remember acts that have been done by others to us and against us.

Once a lady phoned me to say that she was sick and expected to die rather soon. She told me that before she died she wanted something settled. She was sixty-three years old at that time. She told me that when she was twenty years old, she stole ten dollars out of the cash register of a store where she worked. She wanted to send the ten dollars to me and let me return it to the store. Of course, I helped her in every way I could, but imagine the burden of guilt that she had carried for forty-three years for only ten dollars! Why in the name of common sense did she not settle it many years ago? And why in the name of common sense do not all of us settle some things and, like David, "get up and wash our faces" and go on?

Fill Our Minds

The prophet Isaiah promised that "perfect peace" would be the possession of those "whose mind is stayed on thee." I have been saying that we need to *empty* our minds of a lot of things. We also need to *fill* our minds with the right things. Too many of us concentrate on our troubles instead of our triumphs—our problems instead of our powers—our fears instead of our faith—our sins instead of our Saviour.

Once I heard a lady relate that when she went to bed at night, the worries of life would crowd in upon her and she would toss and turn until finally, out of sheer exhaustion, she would go to sleep. In the morning she would wake up tired and nervous. Then one day, she heard or read of a better idea, and she began to practice it with marvelous results. One of her greatest joys was arranging flowers in a vase. She especially liked red roses. When she went to bed at night, she began to picture in her mind a table with two dozen beautiful red roses upon it. In the center of the table she imagined a vase, then mentally, she began picking up the roses one by one, and arranging them in the vase. Usually, she would be asleep before she got all the roses arranged. But that simple little procedure did marvelous things for her.

Here let us read again one of the most psychologically potent statements in all the Bible. "Finally, brethren, whatever is true, whatever is honorable, whatever is just, whatever is pure, whatever is lovely, whatever is gracious, if there is any excellence, if there is anything worthy of praise, think about these things" (Philippians 4:8 RSV).

Ever so often I remind myself of the song which says, "When you are discouraged, thinking all is lost . . . ." Sooner or later, most of us have that experience and then it is we need to remember the next line of that song which is, "Count your many blessings, name them one by one." The Prophet Isaiah said that "perfect peace" is brought about with what we allow to fill our minds.

It is good to think the beautiful things and also our blessings, but the greatest power comes when we begin to fill our minds with God, and that is what Isaiah said: "whose mind is stayed on thee."

Here let me recount a recent and very personal experience. I had a real and a heavy burden on my heart. I could not deal with it as I wanted to, and it worried me considerably. One night I called a close minister friend and said to him, "Would you pray right now over the phone about this problem in my behalf?" He prayed fervently and sincerely, and I said to him that night and I say now, *that the answer came*. I felt the confidence and a joy and a peace. The problem was not a burden any longer. I believe that in that certain circumstance I needed some extra help in letting God become completely dominant in my thinking in reference to that problem. I felt that the answer had come, but I felt completely at ease and at peace. And I realized again the words of Dante, "In His will is our peace." When one makes the commitment to God's will, it leads both to acceptance and to peace.

God's Will

We remember that Christ said, "Nevertheless, not my will, but Thine, be done" (*see* Luke 22:42). When we fill our minds with God to the extent that we accept His will, it brings to us marvelous peace. Yes, Dante said it best: "In His will is our peace." This is true for four reasons.

(1) It takes from us the fear of getting lost in life. I was riding in a small airplane with just the pilot. He let me wear a set of earphones and I could hear distinctly a radio beam. If he turned one direction, there was a different sound; if he turned another direction, still another sound. When he was on course, there was the sound that he wanted to hear. It lead us directly to the airfield to which we wanted to go.

It is fascinating to study the migration of birds. Take for

example the Pacific Golden Plover. These birds are hatched in the northlands of Alaska and Siberia. Before the young ones are old enough to fly great distances, the old birds desert them and fly far away to the Hawaiian Islands. The young birds are left behind to grow strong enough to follow their parents.

One day these birds rise into the sky and set their course over the Pacific. They have never made that journey before, and they must cross two thousand miles of ocean. During this trip they do not have even one opportunity to stop for rest or food, and they frequently encounter high winds and storms. Yet, unerringly they fly straight to those tiny specks in the Pacific, the Hawaiian Islands. How do you explain the flight of those birds? Surely God has provided for those birds something akin to our radio beams—something they can follow without getting lost. And I firmly believe that God has made the same provision for mankind. When our lives are in harmony with God, that is, when we are on "God's beam," we have an instinctive sense of the right direction, and we move forward with courage and confidence without fear of getting lost.

(2) Dante was correct in the second place, because when we commit our lives to God's will, it relieves us of the burden of the responsibility of tomorrow.

Really, it is not our past defeats that make us desperate; it is the fear of the consequences of those defeats tomorrow. We become afraid that we cannot handle the future. But when we become convinced that the future is in God's hands, then our fear is eliminated. God does not usually reveal His will for years ahead. Usually God's will is given us for one step at a time. But that is enough to keep us going.

(3) Commitment to God's will eliminates the conflicts within ourselves. Instead of squandering our energies on countless decisions, we have already made the decision. We have developed a singleness of purpose which gives to us peace and also an unusual strength. There is power in purpose.

(4) There is peace in God's will because it brings to us the approval of a good conscience. I cannot explain exactly what the conscience is or how it works, but I can say that within every one of us there is a voice saying what is right and what is wrong. When we do what God wants us to do, it makes us feel good inside. Really, there is no greater happiness to be found in life than to be able to do what Jesus did when "he lifted his eyes to heaven, and said, 'I have finished the work which thou gavest me to do' " (*see* John 17:1–4). Doing what God wants us to do is really life's greatest happiness.

Let us not be worrying about how to find God's guidance. When we relax our minds in His presence, somehow the guidance comes and we have the assurance. That you can depend on.

The Grief Process

Here is a good place to look again at the grief process most people go through as a result of some defeat, including hurts, and losses, and disappointments. There are times when we wish that we just did not have any feeling at all—but, we really do not mean that. If you were to stick a pin in your finger and did not feel it, that would be much more disturbing to you than the pain which the pin would cause.

Likewise, if some great hurt does not bring you pain, you would be far more disturbed than you are with the pain. Actually, we do not want to lose a sense of feeling.

When the shocking and disturbing experience first happens, there is an immediate reaction. The reaction may vary in different people—some become hysterical and cry; some become angry and curse; some just completely surrender and faint; and some become stoical and make no outward expression at all.

Oftentimes, after a painful experience, a person may feel nothing at all for a period. But later some people begin to play games with themselves, and try to convince themselves that nothing really happened. There are those who have gone on for years and never admitted or faced the reality of the defeat. On the other hand, others reach a moment of emotional cleansing. We do cry, but we also look with joy and thanksgiving that we have had the opportunities which life has given us. In a very real sense many people come to know the meaning of the words of Christ, "Blessed are they that mourn: for they shall be comforted" (Matthew 5:4). Acceptance does lead to peace.

Appreciation

At this point we need to go back and pick up again on a thought mentioned previously in these pages. That is, we need to *express* appreciation. We take too much in life for granted. Express appreciation to God for His blessings; to your wife or husband for what he or she means to you; to the people with whom you work. Never miss an opportunity to make an expression of appreciation for something. Really what life is all about is our relationships—people loving and helping each other—we get and we give—we are thankful. Then we find it easier to accept life, and as we accept life, we find peace.

Here are some words which inspire me:

Celebrate the temporary—
  Don't wait until tomorrow
    Live today.

Celebrate the simple things—
  Enjoy the butterfly
  Embrace the snow
  Run with the ocean
  Delight in the trees

Or a single lonely flower
Go barefoot
  In the wet grass.

Don't wait
  Until all the problems
    Are solved
  Or all the bills
    Are paid.

You will wait forever
Eternity will come and go
  And you
Will still be waiting.

Live in the now
  With all its problems
    And its agonies
  With its joy
    And its pain.

Celebrate your pain—
   Your despair
      Your anger
It means you're alive
   Look closer
   Breathe deeper
   Stand taller
Stop grieving the past.

There is joy and beauty
                    Today
It is temporary
   Here now and gone
So celebrate it
   While you can
Celebrate the tempo-
   rary.

AUTHOR UNKNOWN

8 Try Throwing Your Life

G. A. Studdert-Kennedy was referring to the soldiers who were sitting around the Cross as Jesus was dying. Describing that scene he wrote these wonderful words:

> And sitting down they watched Him there,
> The soldiers did;
> There, while they played with dice,
> He made His sacrifice,
> And died upon the Cross to rid
> God's world of sin.
>
> He was a gambler, too, my Christ,
> He took His life and threw
> It for a world redeemed . . . .
>
> "The Gambler"

One of the tragedies of our present-day society is that we have so perverted the instinct of gambling. Today when we think of gambling we think of casinos, decks of cards, dice, racetracks, and the like. These things are both degrading and sinful. But gambling itself is thrilling, inspiring, and even glorious. I love Studdert-Kennedy's words, "He was a gambler, too, my Christ, He took his life and threw it . . . ." That is the very process of living. Day by day, living demands taking chances and the very act of taking chances means that you are going to win some and lose some. The tragedy comes when we are defeated in some chance experience of life so that we feel defeated in all life and become devastated.

Learn to Live by Faith

One of the great tragedies is to try to eliminate the gambling instinct. When you do that you destroy your soul. We live in a world of uncertainty, even the next minute is hidden from us. We do not know what is going to happen. So, the very act of living requires risk. We must learn to live by faith and not by sight.

One of the things that our age seems to be seeking is security. I pray that we will never have security in this world, because it will destroy all progress in our civilization. Security eliminates the spirit of adventure, and adventure is what sends a Columbus across the Atlantic, or a Lindbergh across that same Atlantic. The world is never built by caution but rather by people who are willing to take chances.

When we are defeated, let us remember that is part of the business of living at its highest. If you never take a chance, you will never be defeated—but you will never accomplish anything either. Also, if you never know defeat, it means that you were never willing to take a chance, and that should make us more devastated than the fact that we *were* defeated. Jesus said, "He that findeth his life shall lose it: and he that loseth his life for my sake shall find it" (Matthew 10:39). If you are defeated in life, most of the time it means that you took a chance. If you are afraid to take a chance and only concerned with saving your life and never tasting defeat, it is a certainty that eventually your defeat will be total and permanent. It is just as much a sin to be too careful as it is to take too many chances.

In the United States today gambling is at an all-time high. There are tremendous gambling resorts that are flourishing. There is more money being bet on horse racing today than ever before in our history. In many ways, great numbers of American people are gambling, but this is the clear indication of our spiritual poverty. It is said that more than 95 percent of all the American people believe in God. The truth is, a large number of people do not believe God makes any difference, and they do not believe God is worth living for. We gamble with cards and dice and betting on horse races because we have no high goals and high purposes to which we are willing to dedicate ourselves. Thus, one of the noblest instincts of mankind becomes perverted and destructive.

Love Takes a Chance

If you are not willing to take a chance on loving somebody, then you will never be hurt, no matter what might happen. If you love a person, then you take the chance of being hurt. If you care nothing for your own life, if you have no dreams and goals and high purposes, then you cannot be defeated. You have surrendered the game before it even started. Let us take defeat as a badge of greatness. The fact that you have been defeated indicates something high and holy and good about you. It was soldier-writer Donald Hankey who said that "Religion is betting one's life there is a God." When you really make that commitment, then you begin to believe in all the high and holy purposes in life. As you believe, you begin to commit yourself, and your life begins to take on meaning and purpose. Then it is that you can be hurt and thwarted and even defeated. I would hate to admit to the fact that I had escaped defeat in life. Sure, defeat is not easy to bear, but an athletic team would never be defeated, if they never went out on the field to play the game. A person will never be defeated who never tries to do anything, or amount to anything. Be glad for your defeats. Quit crying about them. Start shouting praises for them. Without defeats you are nothing.

I do not know who wrote this poem, but I think it is wonderful. It goes like this:

A right good thing is prudence,
And they are useful friends
Who never make beginnings
Before they see the ends;
But give us now and then a man,
And life will crown him king,
Just to take the consequence,
Just to risk the thing.

The trouble with so many people is they believe too little about themselves. We are made for greater things than most of us have ever imagined. We need to take the risk. Surely we can be defeated, but without the possibility of defeat, we also lose the possibility of victory. To become devastated by defeat is to miss the whole purpose and greatness of living!

Here let me quote one of Helen Steiner Rice's poems that I like the best:

Life without purpose
is barren indeed—
There can't be a harvest
unless you plant seed,

There can't be attainment
  unless there's a goal,
And man's but a robot
  unless there's a soul . . .
If we send no ships out,
  no ships will come in,
And unless there's a contest,
  nobody can win . . .
For games can't be won
  unless they are played,
And *Prayers* can't be *answered*
  unless they are *prayed* . . .
So whatever is wrong
  with your life today,
You'll find a solution
  if you kneel down and pray
Not just for pleasure,
  enjoyment and health,
Not just for honors
  and prestige and wealth . . .
But *Pray for a purpose*
  to *make life worth living,*
And *Pray for the Joy*
  of *unselfish giving,*
For *Great is your Gladness*
  and *Rich your Reward*
When you make your *Life's Purpose*
  The choice of the Lord.

Reasons for Living

In my own counseling with many unhappy people who feel defeated and who have given up on life (and given up on themselves), I have suggested they take a sheet of paper and begin writing down some of the reasons for living. We give up and quit because we decide there is no reason for living. Finding a reason for living immediately gives one new power. The best nerve medicine on this earth is a life purpose.

Every so often in my own life, when I have felt discouraged and even defeated, I have turned to the Gospel of John, chapter 20. In that chapter is contained what is to me one of the most heartening stories in all the Bible. The disciples of Jesus had given up everything they had to follow Him. They had even shared in His dreams and in His purposes. Then they had seen Him crucified. They felt that Jesus and all that He stood for, and all to which they had given themselves for, had been completely and utterly defeated. He was crucified on Friday; on Sunday night ten of these disciples were gathered together in some Upper Room. Judas was not with them because he had already given up. Thomas was not with them because he had no faith, but there were ten together. I rather imagine they were there because they were afraid of what might happen to them, and they took some comfort in being with each other.

Into their midst appeared Jesus. He did not condemn them for losing faith; He did not call them cowards for not defending Him from the Cross. In no way did He criticize them. Instead He said, to them, "Peace be unto you: as my Father hath sent me, even so send I you" (v. 21). From that moment on, there is no record that any of those disciples were ever afraid of anything again. They were saved because they were given a purpose. The trouble with so many of us is we emphasize the *defeats* in life instead of defining our *purposes for living*. Unless you have a life purpose, you are not really living.

George Bernard Shaw suggested that an appropriate

epitaph for a lot of people would be ''died at thirty, buried at sixty.'' In contrast, I like the spirit of the old man who said, ''I am going to live until I die, and then I am going to live forever.'' A lot of people worry about the wrong thing. They worry about life after death when they ought to be worrying about life after birth. If a person is properly concerned about living, then he is not improperly worried about eternity.

9 How to Find a Life Purpose

How do I go about finding a life purpose?

One of the first answers to that would be "What do I like most to do?" Really, that involves my desires, my abilities, and my opportunities. I have never used the expressions "sacred" and "secular" in reference to work. To me all work is sacred. Being a good mechanic is just as sacred as is being a good minister. God gave to each of us certain talents and He expects us to use them in some high purpose. To me, one of the saddest verses in all the Bible is: "And I was afraid, and went and hid thy talent in the earth: lo, there thou hast that is thine" (Matthew 25:25). God gives us talents to be *used,* not to be buried, and the very using of our talents carries with it the possibilities of defeat. I keep emphasizing that defeat is a badge of greatness. Nobody wants to lose, but on the other hand, it is a lot worse to bury ourselves and not take any chances or do anything. Defeat is not easy to bear, but not to have the nerve to take the chance that living requires is a lot worse.

There is a legend that once a king placed a heavy stone in the middle of the road. The people who came down that road grumbled about having to walk around that stone. Finally, one man came along, saw the obstacle, and set about the job of moving it. Under the stone he found a purse of gold. So it is in life. Take the chance. For your efforts you may taste disappointment, but you may find gold. It takes faith to commit your life to something, not knowing how it is going to turn out. Those, however, are the people who gain the victories. Remember, every defeat is also a possible victory.

After the death of Mrs. Henry Ford, a newspaper reporter wrote about her with great feeling and understanding. He told about the early days when they had no money at all, yet Mrs. Ford continued to believe in her husband through all of his trials and adversities. Mr. Ford called her "the believer" and in turn she called him "the dreamer." They lived happily together for sixty years. The reporter ended his story with this line: "At last, the believer has gone to rest with the dreamer, two who together are the epitome of the American story." Suppose Mr. and Mrs. Ford had been afraid of defeat! One of our troubles is that we judge life too quickly.

In his book *That Immortal Sea,* Dr. Leslie Weatherhead told the story of a poor native woman in South Africa who was convicted in court for some small offense. She felt completely defeated. Her only possession was one golden coin. Reluctantly, she handed that to the court in payment of her fine. Then a miracle happened. The clerk gave her back in change more money than she thought the coin was worth. What had happened was this: the price of gold had risen since she first acquired the coin. Instead of losing everything, she realized she actually had more left than she thought she had in the first place! Something like that frequently happens to us. In one of many ways we become condemned through some circumstance in life, and we are compelled to pay. We feel that we have lost everything we had, only later to discover that we gained more than we lost.

Humility and Timidity

Through the years I have come to realize that I get humility and timidity mixed up. *Humility* is wonderfully good; *timidity* is defeating and bad. There is no virtue in being "a timid soul." The basis of timidity is that we take ourselves too seriously. Jesus said, "Take no thought for your life . . ." (Matthew 6:25). He is saying that we should quit thinking about ourselves all the time and start thinking about something else. In that same chapter, He says, "Look at the birds . . ." (v. 26 RSV). They do not worry about every daily detail and God takes care of them. He also says, "Look at the wild flowers—the lilies of the field." But God made them beautiful even though they are only to live a short time. Think about how much more God would do for you, who is to live eternally. And Jesus declares that the conclusion of the whole matter is "Seek ye first the kingdom of God . . ." (v. 33). That is, lose yourself in some high holy purpose.

Timidity is nothing but a form of self-reference and egotism. When we quit thinking about ourselves and start thinking about something greater than ourselves, our characters are transformed and we become courageous instead of timid. If you are a shy, timid person, you relate everything to yourself. You are the center of your own thoughts.

Some years ago, a young artist asked me to come and conduct a special service of dedication for a studio she had opened. She told me a wonderful story about herself. When she was a young child, she was severely burned, and it left large and unsightly scars on her face and neck. She became very self-conscious about those scars. She felt that the children at school made unkind remarks about her and she had almost no friendly contacts with other children. During the years, she had several operations seeking to eliminate those scars. Later she went to art school but did not do very well. She believed that her teacher was not interested in her. She became disheartened and discouraged.

Then she told me that one day she read two statements that changed her entire thought processes. She read Paul's statement, "I can do all things through Christ which strengtheneth me" (Philippians 4:13). The other statement was from Ralph Waldo Emerson. He said, "Neither you nor the world knows what you can do until you have tried."

The next day she went to school a different person. Those two statements kept running through her mind. She did more that day than she had been doing. At the close of the class period she was behind a little partition washing out her paint brushes. The teacher did not know she was there, and she heard him say to someone else, "If that girl would only wake up, she could become really a great artist."

She told me that was the most thrilling thing she had ever heard. For the first time she felt somebody had expressed faith in her. The next morning she got to school earlier than she ever had before. She worked harder, she accomplished more, she graduated high in her class. The day we dedicated her studio she said to me, "I have no hesitation in undertaking this studio; I know it will succeed."

Each one of us has something in our lives that is trying to defeat us—that robs us of our power—that makes us shrink back. We can surrender to these things and become another "timid soul." On the other hand, somewhere in life we can find the inspiration to get up and get going. There is such a thing as reaching a point at which we are not worried about whether or not we are defeated. The thing we are concerned about is the feeling that we have tried—and winning or losing is not the most important thing.

Memories Are Good and Bad

When my own mother was eighty-seven years old, she experienced a severe heart attack. For several weeks she was not mentally rational. During these weeks she would constantly talk about the past. One day I said to her, "Mama, you are in the hospital; how do you suppose you got here?"

Her reply was, "Why, Mr. Ledford brought me in his wagon." Mr. Ledford lived in her community when she was a child. Undoubtedly he had a wagon and she had ridden in it sometime, somewhere, maybe a number of times. Mr. Ledford died when my mother was ten years old. But in her present mental state, she was living more than seventy-five years ago.

That is an illustration of what can happen to a lot of people. Under the shock of some unhappy experience we can spend our time living in the past.

A lot of people enjoy talking about the so-called "good old days," when there were less crime, less problems, and less worries. We enjoy nostalgia and memory is one of the great blessings of humanity.

I know a man who had a stroke. It severely curtailed his memory. One day he showed me his workshop. It was filled with beautiful woodworking tools. Throughout his house was lovely furniture that he had made. Very sadly he told me that he could not use the tools any more because he had completely forgotten how. That part of his memory tape was completely erased by the stroke. We do want to look back and remember, but we need to remind ourselves that the past is past. In our memories, we not only enjoy many things, but we also suffer much. We remember thoughts and words and deeds that we wish we had never had. We remember failures and defeats with sorrow and disappointment. Let us also remember that once Jesus said to a man, "Ye must be born again." One of the things that statement means is that we do not need to live in the past. We can also live in the future. As we think about it, surely the future is much more exciting than the past.

Before I Sleep

As I sit writing these words, I remember very vividly about a time when I was in the hospital. I had had a minor operation and I felt that it would amount to very little. But somehow an infection developed and for a time the doctors could not determine exactly what the infection was and what antibiotic I needed. I became the sickest I had ever been in my life. I never shall forget one Saturday afternoon about three o'clock. I was listening over the radio to a football game. I began to feel worse than I had felt earlier. I believed that I was dying. Later the doctor confirmed the fact that at that time I was at my lowest point. I remember thinking that I did not want to die listening to the football game, so I turned off the radio and began thinking about my family, my life, and most especially, about what the future might hold for me. During that time, one of the poems of Robert Frost came to my mind. It was a poem that I had memorized many years ago, but I could not seem to remember it.

I remembered the occasion of the poem. He was driving his horse through a particularly beautiful grove of trees. It was snowing and it was a lovely scene. He felt like just staying there and watching the beauty. As I thought of that scene the last lines of the poem came back to me and I kept repeating them over and over and over to myself. They go like this:

> But I have promises to keep,
> And miles to go before I sleep,
> And miles to go before I sleep.

Somehow those words kept going over and over in my mind. I really believe they meant the difference in my living and dying. With those words in my mind, I could not give up. I began thinking of things I needed to do, that my life was not finished, and that there was more to live for. I did not realize that at that very moment there were a number of people in the laboratory, analyzing my blood, seeking the exact infection I had. One of the laboratory technicians is a very skilled lady who sings in the choir of the church where I am the pastor. She told me how they diligently studied my blood samples and suddenly one of them said, "Here it is." Immediately, they got a specific antibiotic and brought it to my room and began letting it flow into my veins. Within the space of two hours, I felt completely different. I knew that life could go on. When I got home I looked up the poem and now I have read it many, many times. I really think it saved my life. Here is the entire poem.

"Stopping by Woods on a Snowy Evening"

> Whose woods these are I think I know.
> His house is in the village though;
> He will not see me stopping here
> To watch his woods fill up with snow.

My little horse must think it queer
To stop without a farmhouse near
Between the woods and frozen lake
The darkest evening of the year.

He gives his harness bells a shake
To ask if there is some mistake.
The only other sound's the sweep
Of easy wind and downy flake.

The woods are lovely, dark and deep.
But I have promises to keep,
And miles to go before I sleep,
And miles to go before I sleep.

ROBERT FROST

10 We Need to Believe

When we think of the words of Studdert-Kennedy: "He took his life and threw it," and when we think of throwing our own lives into a dim, unknown future, we need faith. Faith is based on belief. Again and again, I have talked to defeated, unhappy people about what they believe. If we can assert our beliefs, most of the time that will be the power we need to keep on living.

Sometime ago, I asked myself the question, "What do I really believe?" In the answer to that question, I wrote a book entitled *What I Have Lived By*. Fleming H. Revell published the book and I am very happy that it is now having a large sale in the bookstores across the country. But really, I did not write that book thinking about its sale. I wrote it thinking about the future living of my own life. Reaffirming my own beliefs gave me strength that I need. That is true of every one of us. That is why I constantly say to defeated people, "Tell me some things that you believe."

At this point, I do not intend to summarize my own beliefs, but from my counseling experiences I would like to lift up some of the things that people have said to me.

What They Believe In

One man who felt that life had treated him badly said, "The highest belief I have is that God is like Jesus. Believing that, I can go on living." Another man said to me, "Every Sunday I attend the church service. I find myself sitting with a group of people; I listen to the choir; I sing the hymns; I join in the responses and prayers of the service; I hear the sermon. When I leave the church I feel stronger and better able to face the coming week." For many people the church is not important, but at least this one man found it important enough to keep his life going.

Another person put it this way, "For me, life is a pilgrimage. It is not a pleasure party and I do not expect that the chief reward of life is pleasure. I know that there are hard places in the road to travel, but I believe that the road of life leads somewhere. Exactly where that is and what it is, I am not sure, but I am determined to keep going as far as I can in the pilgrimage of life."

Another said, "When I come to the end of life, the question I will be asking myself is, 'Well, what did you make of it?' To me this is the entire meaning of life. I have one chance, and I am determined to make something out of it, in spite of difficulties and hardships." Along that same line, another person put it this way: "To me, life is achieving. Not achieving in a sense of things done and the amount of money I accumulate—in the honors I receive—but rather in achieving in the sense of being a real person."

Paul Tillich, the eminent theologian, declared: "Just in this situation where God is far from our consciousness, where we are unable to pray or experience any meaning in life, God's spirit is working quietly in our souls. In the moment when we feel separated from God, meaningless in our lives, and condemned to despair, suddenly we know that we are not alone."

A friend of mine put it this way: "Every so often the words come to my mind 'Is it nothing to you—all ye who pass by?' And then I think of Isaiah who faced the same challenge and responded, 'Here am I, Lord, send me.' That gets me going again when I feel low and useless and worthless."

Another person explained it: "I believe that God is love and when a person loves, he or she knows the larger part of God. Whether one knows love in a family relationship, in a friendship, in deep concern for the needs of others—no matter what circumstance—I know that if I will keep on loving then I will know God. I know that the greatest and most important fact of life is the reality of God. Knowing there is a God, I can keep on keeping on."

Beginner's Creed

Dr. Clarence J. Forsberg, pastor of the Missouri United Methodist Church in Columbia, Missouri, said it as well as it can be said; "I know that this is not going to satisfy everyone, or put all your questions to rest. It is not intended as a definitive creed. All that I want to do is to suggest a right place to begin. If you are one of those who needs such a place, then let me suggest this as a beginner's creed: *Life is worth living, people are worth loving, and God is worth trusting.*"

11 Learn Forgiveness—Forgetting

I now spend my vacations going several times a year with small groups to the Holy Land. Each year we take two or three trips over there, and each night I lecture about the life of our Lord. One of the places that we visit which we feel is most authentic is Jacob's Well. On our tours I talk about the problems of the woman that Jesus met at the well and how He helped her. She was a Samaritan and Jews looked down upon Samaritans as inferior people. Not only that, she had had a sordid past, but from her Jesus took water to quench His thirst, and to her He gave new inspiration for life.

To begin with, He accepted her as a person. Most of us remember with sorrow some times when we did not feel accepted and we can remember how hurt we were. On the other hand, most of us remember when we failed to accept another person, and we deeply regret the sorrow it might have caused.

Many years ago, I was preaching for several nights in the Mulberry Street Methodist Church in Macon, Georgia. Across the street from the church is a lovely little park. One night before the service, I was sitting out in that park alone, thinking about my sermon and watching the people going into the church.

As I was sitting there, a black woman and a little boy came walking down the sidewalk. I assumed he was her son and he appeared about five years old. As they got to the park he ran in and sat down in one of the swings and began to swing himself.

His mother came over and got him by the arm. She said to him, "You can't swing in that swing."

He asked, "Why can't I swing in that swing?"

She replied, "That swing is for white children."

As they walked out of the park, I could hear his reply, and the words of that little boy have rung in my ears ever since. Very plaintively he said to his mother, "Mama, I wish I was a white child."

I knelt by the bench upon which I was sitting and I prayed, "Oh, God, the remainder of my life help me to do everything I possibly can to give that little boy the chance to swing in that swing."

We Need to Forgive

One of the places we need to begin our forgiving is in our relationships with other people. We have prejudice and we have experienced prejudice. Jesus made that Samaritan woman feel she was somebody. We need to forgive the people we have hurt. Oftentimes we hold resentments against the person that *we* have wronged more than against a person who has wronged *us*.

One of the things Jesus did for this woman was, He allowed her to do something for Him. Many times we need help, but are not willing to accept it from others. It takes grace to give and grace to receive. We need food to eat and water to drink; we need rest when the day is done; and when we are lonely we need friendly companionship. There are many needs in our lives that others can meet. One of the ways to help people is, right at this point, to be willing to accept somebody else's help. In the second place, Jesus ministered to her. He was willing to talk about the future instead of the past. Her life was changed, and it all came about because Jesus was willing to say to a Samaritan woman, "Would you please give Me a drink of water?"

It has been said that Robert Louis Stevenson once tried to pray the Lord's Prayer, but he got up from his knees and said, "I cannot pray it." He did not feel that he could forgive some people and those words, "Forgive us our trespasses as we forgive those who trespass against us" were his stumbling block.

He is not the only person who has had problems with this petition in the Lord's Prayer. The truth is, every one of us has somebody we need to forgive—but find it difficult.

The Debts We Owe

One of the most helpful experiences for any of us is to list some of the debts that we owe. My mind goes back to a very early time in my ministry, when my wife and I first started. We had very little money and we bought things on credit, such as groceries. We bought a car and agreed to pay twenty-five dollars a month. Paying for that car gave me my most vivid idea of eternity. I thought we would never complete the payments, but finally we did. Then a marvelous thing happened in our lives. We sat down and talked about our money and we decided two things: First, that we would give one-tenth of everything the church paid us back to the church. There have been times when we did not have enough to eat, when the best clothes we had were patched, but there has never been a time from that day until this day, when we used the Lord's money on ourselves. The second thing we agreed on was that from that day on, we would never buy anything on credit. We have stuck by that also. If we did not have the money, we have done without, and it is amazing how much one can do without. From that day, we have lived without debt.

On the other hand, every day of my life I have gone deeper in debt, because I cannot remember a day when somebody has not done something good for me, or, in some way I have not used the contributions of other people to make my life better. As I write these words, I am using an electric light. I did not discover electricity or learn how to make a light bulb. I am indebted to Thomas Edison. When I get in my car, I am indebted to those who made it and the mechanics who keep it operating. When I eat food or wear clothes, I am indebted to those who made it possible. As I list those to whom I am in debt, I name my wife, my children, my parents, my ancestors, my teachers, my friends, the members of my church, even strangers I have met along the way. There is no way that I can completely list all of my debts. Financially I have paid my way, but when it comes to life, I have lived on credit. I owe debts to people beyond my imagination.

Also, I think back with joy and appreciation of the loving parents and brothers and sisters I had. There were seven children in our family, and through the years, there has been the fellowship of love among us. I think about how my own family overlooked my faults and my wrongs and loved me in spite of myself.

One could write at great length at this point, but when we think of our own need of forgiveness, it really becomes easy to forgive other people. Holding a grudge—not being willing to forgive—is very unbecoming of any reasonable person.

Our Own Guilts

As we think of forgiveness we think of our own guilts. Everyone has a conviction of having done wrong. We do wrong today; we did wrong yesterday; we have done wrong as far back as we can remember. This sense of guilt is self-destructive, because it threatens our self-esteem and fills us with anxiety. The feeling of not being right is a depressing feeling. The good news is that God understands our humanness, that God accepts us, He loves us and that He forgives us. What is the most beautiful color in the world? When we see a gorgeous sunset, surely we would say it is crimson. When we look at the blue of the ocean, or the green of a valley, or the purple of a violet—in each instance, we would choose that color. But as was mentioned before, we agree with G. K. Chesterton, who said, "God paints in many colors, but He never paints so gorgeously as when He paints in white."

We think of the words of the prophet Isaiah, "Though your sins be as scarlet, they shall be as white as snow" (Isaiah 1:18). There is no promise in the Bible more welcome and more glorious than that promise. And it is given to each and every one of us. My plea is *that we accept it*.

The proof that we believe in the forgiveness of God is in forgiving ourselves. If we do not forgive ourselves, then we do not believe God has forgiven us. We have the promise of His forgiveness. *Believe* it, *accept* it, and *look for* it.

There is a story of a physician whose books were examined after he died. It was discovered that a number of the accounts were crossed out and the doctor had written across the page: FORGIVEN—TOO POOR TO PAY. The physician's wife decided that many of these people *could* pay, and so she took some of these accounts to court. The judge asked one question: "Is this your husband's handwriting?" When she replied that it was, he said: "Then there is no tribunal in the land that can obtain this money, when he has written the word *forgiven*." That story comes from the pen of Emery Park and is quoted by Charles Wallace in one of his books. But really, that story comes from the heart of God. When God says it is forgiven, then it *is* forgiven, and there is no guilt and no liability any longer.

Forget Past Failures

I used to preach a sermon entitled "Forget Past Failures—Success Lies Ahead." I am sure that is not original with me and that many ministers have used that title. It has been a number of years since I preached that sermon, and I did not bother to look up my notes. Really, I feel no need to preach the sermon here. Just the title is enough of a reminder. There is a sense in which we never forget anything. But this is the type of forgetting I am now talking about: when we can reach the place where we do not remember with guilt, or regret, or with shame.

Here let me repeat a good story. Two old friends met up with each other late one afternoon downtown. They had not seen each other in many years, and so they decided to have dinner together. They sat and they talked, remembering all the happy experiences of many years ago. Finally, one of them realized that it was three o'clock in the morning. With one accord, each said, "We must hurry home."

The next day they met again and one said to the other, "How did your wife take your coming in so late last night?"

The man replied, "I explained to her, she understood, and it was perfectly all right. How did your wife react?"

The man replied, "When I got home, my wife became historical."

The friend replied, "You mean hysterical."

The other man said, "No, I mean historical. She brought up everything that had happened in the last thirty years."

As I tell the above story, really I feel a bit of a sense of guilt, because men are more apt to bring up the past than are women. Women find it easier to forgive than men do, but even so, there comes a time when we need to quit being "historical."

That does not mean that we ought to forget everything. As I have mentioned previously in these pages, we do owe debts beyond number to other people and to society. But there is an area where we need to say with Saint Paul, ". . . forgetting those things which are behind, and reaching forth unto those things which are before" (Philippians 3:13).

12 You Have to Have Faith

Faith fits right in at this point. I have never known it to be described better than by Studdert-Kennedy. His poem-essay entitled "Faith" is one that I have read again and again through the years. Let's read it again right now:

FAITH

How do I know that God is good? I don't.
I gamble like a man. I bet my life
Upon one side in life's great war. I must,
I can't stand out. I must take sides. The man
Who is a neutral in this fight is not
A man. He's bulk and body without breath,
Cold leg of lamb without mint sauce. A fool.
He makes me sick. Good Lord! Weak tea!
        Cold slops!
I want to live, live out, not wobble through
My life somehow, and then into the dark.
I must have God. This life's too dull without,
Too dull for aught but suicide. What's man
To live for else? I'd murder someone just
To see red blood. I'd drink myself blind drunk
And see blue snakes if I could not look up
To see blue skies, and hear God speaking through
The silence of the stars. How is it proved?
It isn't proved, you fool, it can't be proved.

How can you prove a victory before
It's won? How can you prove a man who leads,
To be a leader worth the following,
Unless you follow to the death—and out
Beyond mere death, which is not anything
But Satan's lie upon eternal life?
Well—God's my leader, and I hold that He
  is good, and strong enough to work His plan
And purpose out to its appointed end.
I am no fool, I have my reasons for
This faith, but they are not the reasonings,
The coldly calculated formula
Of thought divorced from feeling. They are true,
Too true for that. There's no such thing as thought
Which does not feel, if it be real thought.
And not thought's ghost—all pale and sicklied o'er
With dead conventions—abstract truth—man's lie
Upon this living, loving, suff'ring Truth,
That pleads and pulses in my very veins,
The blue blood of all beauty, and the breath
  of life itself. I see what God has done,
What life in this world is. I see what you
See, this eternal struggle in the dark.
I see the foul disorders, and the filth
Of mind and soul, in which men, wallowing
Like swine, stomp on their brothers till they drown
In puddles of stale blood, and vomitings
Of their corruption. This life stinks in places,
'Tis true, yet scent of roses and of hay
New mown comes stealing on the evening breeze,
  and through the market's din, the bargaining
  of cheats, who make God's world a den of thieves,
I hear sweet bells ring out to prayer, and see
The faithful kneeling by the Calvary of Christ.

I walk in crowded streets where men
And women, mad with lust, loose-lipped and lewd,
Go promenading down to hell's wide gates;
Yet have I looked into my mother's eyes,
And seen the light that never was on sea
Or land, the light of Love, pure Love and true,
And on that Love I bet my life. I back
My mother 'gainst a whore when I believe
In God, and can a man do less or more?
I have to choose. I back the scent of life
Against its stink. That's what Faith works out at
Finally. I know not why the Evil,
I know not why the Good, both mysteries
Remain unsolved, and both insoluble.
I know that both are there, the battle set,
And I must fight on this side or on that.
I can't stand shiv'ring on the bank, I plunge
Head first. I bet my life on Beauty, Truth,
And Love, not abstract but incarnate Truth,
Not Beauty's passing shadow but its Self.
Its very Self made flesh, Love realized.
I bet my life on Christ—Christ Crucified.

. . . .

Doubts About God

As we discuss faith, we come to the question of our belief in God. There is a verse which I have often read and most of us have experienced in some moment of life, ". . . The Lord said that he would dwell in the thick darkness" (1 Kings 8:12). I am reminded of how the great Harry Emerson Fosdick once began a sermon in the Riverside Church in New York. He said:

> Once more today I feel what I commonly feel when I face worshiping congregations. You look so pious. You are so

reverent. You listen so respectfully to Scripture and anthem. You sing so earnestly the resounding hymns. But I know and you know that in every life there is something else which our worship does not express—doubts, questions, incertainties, skepticism. Every one of us, facing the Christian faith, must honestly say what the man in the gospel story said to Jesus, ". . . Lord, I believe; help thou mine unbelief" (Mark 9:24).

Four Thoughts About God

In reference to our doubts about God, let me make several observations. First, doubt is not a sin. If you read the autobiographies of even the greatest saints, you will find them expressing doubts from time to time. Christ did not condemn Thomas for his doubts.

A second fact about God is that He seems so far away. As children we grew up with the idea that God was way off up yonder or out yonder somewhere.

In the third place, we deal with the silence of God. As Jesus was hanging on the Cross, God did not say a word and He was moved to cry out, ". . . My God, my God, why hast thou forsaken me?" (Matthew 27:46). And in the midst of our crosses we do not hear God's voice and our faith is shaken.

A fourth problem we have is that we have no vocabulary with which we can adequately talk about God. With our very limited knowledge, there is no way that we can intelligently discuss an infinite God. This leaves us frustrated and confused.

Practical Atheism

An increasing problem in our society today is practical atheism. Intellectually, we admit to the existence of God, but really we do not believe God makes any difference. Certainly in the United States the term "secular cities" is becoming more and more real. It is a fact that the more prosperous a society is, the less need that society feels for God. We become self-sufficient and God becomes completely irrelevant. The United States is rapidly becoming, for all practical purposes, an atheistic society in which more and more people believe they can get along without God.

One other problem in our society today is our vast knowledge. In civilizations in the long ago, everything was attributed to God. In their ignorance, disease, disaster, death were all from God's hand. But in our age of enlightenment, we now can explain everything apart from God and we have about decided we know about all there is to know.

But when we sincerely open our hearts to God, when we reach the point that we are willing to be obedient to Him, and when we really believe that Jesus Christ is God in Person, then faith becomes true power in our lives.

13 The Church Bids You to Look Up

The greatest event in human history is not when man walked on the moon. The greatest event in human history is when God walked on the earth.

With his magnificent pictures, Norman Rockwell has interpreted life for at least two generations of America. In one of his last illustrations, he pictured throngs of people passing by the open door of a beautiful church. The people are going by with heads down and downcast eyes. All they are seeing is a narrow strip of sidewalk stretching before them. Over the door of the cathedral are the words LIFT UP THINE EYES.

Hubert Humphrey was so impressed with what Norman Rockwell had done that he wrote an article and entitled it "Four Words to Remember." Today, we desperately need the message of the church, which is LIFT UP THINE EYES. Recently I had lunch with a minister who had just celebrated his thirty-fifth anniversary as pastor of the largest church in a city. I asked him what were the most significant changes he has seen during those thirty-five years. He told me that thirty-five years ago, 65 percent of the people in that city went to church. Today, he said 40 percent of the people of that city go to church. My own feeling is, he is too optimistic. I doubt if there is a major city in America today where more than a third of the people ever go to church. This is a tragedy. One of the reasons that many people feel devastated by defeat is they do not have the inner resources they would find in church.

Reasons to Attend

Let me very quickly give some reasons why I believe a person should regularly attend worship in some church. The first reason is that being in church identifies you as a child of God. It makes you realize that you are more than just a mortal being. You are immortal.

Another value of the church is that it gives inspiration to live because it gives us true meanings about what life really is. Life can become dull and monotonous, but the church reminds us that we are creatures above the monotony. Some time ago, I was reading a sermon by Frank K. Bostian, which appeared in the July, 1971 issue of *Pulpit Preaching*. He told this story: Hallas Elliott Kirk prepared a sermon on the theme "Castles in Spain." He wanted to describe the architectural beauties of those castles and share with his congregation some of the joys and values of his recent journey to that country. As the service began, he looked over the congregation and saw in her usual pew near the front, an Irish woman, who made her living scrubbing clothes over a washboard. He asked himself, *What will she care about these castles in Spain?* Then he wished that he had thought of her before he had prepared this sermon. But it was too late to make a change now. He noticed that this lady seemed to keep her eyes on him and to be taking every word with eagerness. When she clasped his hand at the door, she said, "Thank you for that sermon this morning.

Those 'castles in Spain' made me forget those dirty washtubs."

Self-centeredness

Lift up thine eyes. We need something in our society to get our eyes off the sidewalks and into the heavens—an institution that teaches us what's important in life—an institution dedicated to helping build a better society. The tragedy of too many people is that they are too self-centered.

A man was shaving and he got to looking at his own face. He said to his wife, "You know I am not really very good-looking." His wife made a wonderful reply. She said, "No people are good-looking when they are just looking at themselves." That's the trouble with a lot of people. We never see anybody but ourselves. The church causes us to realize that we are a part of a fellowship and a brotherhood within the Christian church. The hymn "Blest Be the Tie That Binds Our Hearts in Christian Love" is very real. It is an experience that many of us constantly feel within the church.

Every so often, people remind me of what the church asks them to give. My reply is "God is not going to let anybody outgive Him."

Quotable Quotes

In keeping the faith, the church is a great ally. I quoted from a sermon by Frank K. Bostian, which appeared in the July 1971 issue of *Pulpit Preaching.* In that same issue there are two wonderful stories which I feel have a lot to do with faith. One comes from Robert W. Olewiler, quoting John Arthur Gossip:

> The flame of worship has sunk so low and burns so dimly that many nowadays either never think of practicing the presence of God or do so only in a perfunctory fashion.
>
> We need the Sunday bath just as much as the proverbial Saturday night one. Our souls, in daily contact with influences less than perfect, get dirty, too. Cleanliness results from renewing our fellowship with God, revitalizing our principles, and strengthening our convictions. That's why there's a Sunday in the week.
>
> We must nourish the roots of faith before we can expect the fruits of action. Before there is perspiration from work, there must be inspiration from worship, the word that can change your life.

The other comes from Harold Blake Walker:

> "A Canticle for Leibowitz" is an imaginative story of those trying to rebuild from the ruins of nuclear destruction after years of desolation. As the scholars of the Albertian Order of Leibowitz seek to reconstruct the nature of civilization before the disaster, like contemporary archeologists seeking to recover understanding of ancient times, one scholar says to another, "I can't accept it." He cannot believe the legend of man's former attainments. "How can a great and wise civilization have destroyed itself so completely?" The scholar beside him replied, "Perhaps by being materially great and materially wise, nothing else."

One of Dr. Norman Vincent Peale's favorite sayings is "Try faith and watch what happens."

Forgiveness takes away the guilt. *Forgetting* takes away the obsession. *Faith* gives us the power to start over and to keep going. *Forgiveness—Forgetting—Faith*—when the three of them start working together, powerful forces come into our lives, and wonderful things happen. We do not need to be devastated by our defeats.

14 No Matter What Happens—Keep on Believing

There is a phrase in the Book of Zechariah in the Bible which gives me strength and comfort. It is: "Turn you to the strong hold, ye prisoners of hope . . ." (9:12). To me that phrase means that in spite of our limitations or cruel circumstances under which we are compelled to live, or the bed of pain in which one must lie; despite crippled bodies, or lack of money, or many other handicaps—even though we are locked inside the prison walls of seeming defeat—we are not really prisoners of those defeats because, to the contrary, we are "prisoners of hope." You can't be a prisoner of defeat and a prisoner of hope at the same time. The truth of the matter is, seeming defeats are the breeding grounds of strong and vibrant hopes: Hopes that possess us, that drive us, that will not let us quit.

In the sport of boxing, there is an expression "throwing in the towel." That means that when a boxer seems hopelessly defeated but still fighting, his manager will throw a towel in the ring signifying surrender and the end of the fight. But in life, we who are "prisoners of hope" never throw in the towel because defeat is never final.

The trouble with a lot of people is that they let themselves get imprisoned by defeat, because they never speak up or do anything. I am reminded of something the great Reverend Martin Niemöller said. He was a prominent Protestant minister in Germany when Hitler came to power. In seeking to explain the ineffectiveness of the church in thwarting the inhumane treatment by the Nazi regime, he said this:

> In Germany, the Nazis first came for the Communists, and I didn't speak up because I was not a Communist. Then they came for the Jews, and I did not speak up because I was not a Jew. Then they came for trade unionists, and I didn't speak up because I wasn't a trade unionist. Then they came for the Catholics, and I was a Protestant, so I didn't speak up. Then they came for me . . . . By that time there was no one to speak up for anyone.

You never win by surrender; you win by believing there is something that can be done and doing it.

As I read my mail one morning recently, there were five letters in that one mail from people who are prisoners of defeat. One was from a wife whose husband is insanely jealous. They have four children. He does not want her ever to leave the house, even to go to church. She is finding life unbearable.

Another letter was from a schoolteacher who said she could hardly bear the thought of beginning school the next week and facing a room of adolescents day after day. She was tired of teaching but could not find anything else to do.

The third letter was from a wife whose husband is good and kind until he starts drinking. Then he is very cruel, and in these drunken fits she and the children are badly mistreated.

The next letter was from a mother whose only son is

planning to marry soon, and she feels that the girl that he is marrying is a very unfortunate choice. Reading her letter, I am inclined to agree with her.

The last letter was from an eighteen-year-old girl telling me about her marriage, which was a sad mistake. Now, the boy she married has walked out and left her with a baby. He cannot support them, and she does not know anyone to turn to. She frantically wonders what she should do.

Worrying Into Helplessness

Day by day I get letters such as these. To begin with, people can just worry themselves into helplessness. In the words of a popular song of some years ago, people become "bewitched, bothered, and bewildered." But that does not get you anywhere.

Neither does it help our situations to just complain and protest. We can ask a thousand times *Why?* We can say that life is mistreating us, and we can become bitter and moody. But that does not do any good.

We can give up, lose heart, forget our dreams, and spend our days in a drab, miserable existence.

Be Honest With Yourself

As I communicate with people who have problems in life, there are three suggestions that I have: First, be honest with yourself. Many times we cry out against the circumstances of life when really the fault is within us. Many times we say the situation is hopeless, when really it is we ourselves who are hopeless. I think often of the story of the man who was moving. As he entered the new community where he was to live, he asked the first person he met what kind of people lived there.

This person made a very astute reply. He said, "What kind of people lived in the community where you have just come from?"

The man replied, "They were fussing, narrow-minded, disagreeable people, and that is the reason I moved from that community."

"Well," the other man replied, "you will find the same kind of people in this community."

Most of us pretty much find what we are looking for, and the situations and the people are oftentimes the mirror of our own attitudes and our own feelings. I am not suggesting that the fault is always in us. But I am suggesting, in the words of the old spiritual, "It's not my brother, not my sister, but it's me, O Lord, standing in the need of prayer." The place to begin changing the situation is within ourselves. We usually find the kind of people and the kind of circumstances that we are looking for.

Take an Objective Attitude

Second, I tell people to take an objective attitude toward every situation in life. Stop and analyze the facts of the case. Through the years of my ministry, I have counselled with numerous people. I use two questions. First: *What is your situation?* Sometimes it takes a good deal of probing and discussion, but there is marvelous power in understanding really what the problem is. Then I ask my second question: *What do you think you ought to do about it?* Nearly every time, the person comes up with a good answer.

You Are Not Alone

Third, I say to people, *Know that you are not alone.* There is a story that I have heard often of two men who were riding together. One of them was busy working a crossword puzzle. He turned to his friend and asked, "What is a word of three letters, with the letter *O* in the middle, meaning man's best friend?" His friend replied, "Dog." The word *dog* did not fit into the puzzle. The man kept working at it, and then turned to his friend and said, "The last letter of that word is *D*." But still they couldn't quite figure out the word. They never did come up with the answer that the first letter of that word is *G*. And in the situations of life there are numbers of people who never come to realize that our best friend *is* GOD.

First, be honest with yourself; second, understand the situation; third, in the words of the psalmist, ". . . hope thou in God . . ." (Psalms 42:5). As long as you believe in God you are a "prisoner of hope." The most profane word in the English language is the word *hopeless,* because to use that word is to deny the existence, the power, the presence, and the love of Almighty God.

15 Defeats May Be Your Greatest Blessings

In the Book of Hebrews we read, "If ye endure chastening, God dealeth with you as with sons . . ." (12:7). That is, the pathway to the closest relationship with God is through "chastening"—hardships, difficulties, problems, doubts, and even defeats.

More Receptive

Defeat can be a blessing for three reasons. First, it makes us more receptive to God. One of the greatest ministers I have ever known was Dr. Pierce Harris. He and I were close friends, and from him I learned many things. As I mentioned earlier, one of the expressions that he often used was "It is difficult to hold a full cup steady—especially if it has been suddenly filled." What he is saying is that prosperity can throw us out of balance. We become self-sufficient, self-centered, and selfish. On the other hand, I cannot think of any really great person who has not suffered some defeat. When you talk of great persons, let's talk about one of the greatest who ever lived. His name was Moses. Moses was reared in the lap of luxury and ease. His slightest wish was granted. But one day he lost his temper.

He saw an Egyptian mistreating one of the Hebrews, and angrily he killed the Egyptian, buried his body, and thought no one would ever know. But his secret was discovered, and he had to flee the country. Surely he felt bitterness and disappointment in losing his position and all the luxuries of life. He was forced to become a lowly sheepherder. Surely he was a man with a chastened spirit.

However, one day out on the range as he was watching the sheep, he saw a bush on fire. The bush kept burning but never burned up. He went over to the bush, and he realized he was in God's presence. He even pulled off his shoes because it was holy ground, and there he heard the voice of God sending him back to Egypt to face up to Pharaoh. Out of that experience came his greatest victories, even the very foundations of our society today. Had not Moses been defeated, he never would have become great.

It is during times of defeat that we see the "burning bushes."

More Resourceful

Second, defeats cause us to discover our real selves. The great Booker T. Washington used to speak of the "advantage of a disadvantage." He himself was a pioneer example. As a slave boy, he was forced to carry the books of his white master's children to school. He wanted to go to school, too, but the doors were closed to him. Early in life he felt the spirit of defeat, but he developed a passion for an education, and he became one of the best-educated men of his day.

You never discover what you really can do, until you need to do it.

There is no Christian minister who has inspired more people than the great Dr. Norman Vincent Peale. When I was a young preacher, barely making a living in the mountains of North Georgia, I borrowed money for a plane trip to New York just to get to meet Dr. Peale. He talked to me for two hours, and I feel that his touch that day upon my life—and many times since—has been a great blessing. I love and appreciate this man who has given his life in making defeated people feel that they should keep going.

One of the stories that Dr. Peale told was about a friend of his named Webb Young. Webb Young grew beautiful apples, and he advertised them to a very select clientele as "perfect." One year just before time to harvest his apples, a heavy hail storm came. It did not harm the apples, but it left unsightly brown spots upon them. He felt hopelessly defeated. He could not afford to send his apples out with those spots upon them. A lesser man would have given up, but he kept thinking until he possessed a saving idea.

He harvested the apples and packed them in boxes, as he normally did. Then in each box he placed a card which he had had printed. He stated that these apples are grown in high altitude, and he explained that the chill of the mountains makes the apples firm. He also explained that in these high altitudes they often have hail storms. Then he said that if one will look closely at the apples, hail marks upon them can be observed. It is a matter of record that the next year the overwhelming majority of his orders were for "hail-marked" apples. The blemishes became assets.

More Redemptive

Third, defeats make us redemptive.

It has been quoted many times, but it seems fitting for me to put right here, again, the story of a man whose mother died when he was a child.

- Years later he ran for the state legislature—but was defeated.
- He entered business—but a worthless partner put him into bankruptcy.
- He fell deeply in love with a girl—but she died.
- He served one term in Congress—but was defeated for reelection.
- He tried for an appointment to the U.S. Land Office—but failed to get it.
- He sought to be a lyceum lecturer—but failed.
- He ran for the United States Senate—but was defeated.
- He ran for vice-president of the United States of America—but was defeated.
- He was killed by an assassin's bullet.
- His name was Abraham Lincoln.

As we study the life of Lincoln, it is easy to believe that defeats can be redeeming.

Earlier, I quoted from chapter 12 of the Book of Hebrews. Let us go back to that chapter again, and read the first and second verses, in which we find these words: ". . . let us run with patience the race that is set before us, Looking unto Jesus the author and finisher of our faith; who for the joy that was set before him . . . ."

How does that verse continue? Does it say, "Looking unto Jesus . . . who was the greatest teacher of all times"?

Does it say, "Looking unto Jesus, who was the most successful leader of men"?

Does it say, "Looking unto Jesus, who enjoyed all of the favors of Almighty God"?

As we read, we see it says, "Looking unto Jesus . . . who . . . endured the cross . . . ." We need to remind ourselves that crosses can be defeating, but not necessarily so. Crosses have the power to make us more receptive to God, more resourceful, more redemptive.

16 Changes May Be Good

One of the constant problems we face is the problem of change. Really, we should not link the two words—problems and change—together but we do. For most of us, change is a problem. In the well-known hymn "Abide With Me" we sing the words, "Change and decay in all around I see." We link "change" and "decay" together. There is a tendency to feel that change is bad.

I heard a minister say recently, "Since I have been in the church, there have been a lot of changes, and I have been opposed to all of them." The truth of the matter is, most people oppose most changes. Someone wrote this:

> Come weal, come woe
> My status is quo.

However, the old worn-out phrase is still true: "We live in a world of change." There are changes in our political system, and we divide politically pretty much on the basis of those in favor of change and those in favor of no change. A list of changes in our society would be utterly endless. We have seen tremendous transformations in the emergence of a multiracial society. Attitudes of the college campus are not the same as they used to be. In the great industries of our nation there is change in the employer-employee relationships. We see changes in the status of women, in family patterns, in attitudes toward authority, in scientific discoveries, and on and on.

However, most of us have come to realize that we live in an evolving world, and that change is the very essence of things. The problem for most of us is when change comes into our own lives. It is hard to think of anything about us becoming different, but changes do come, and when they come, many of us feel defeated. We want to keep things as they always have been, but children have a way of growing up and leaving home.

As we grow older, we assume different positions in society: a husband or a wife can die; a divorce can take place; our jobs can be radically changed.

Instead of a defensive attitude toward change, we need to let the gospel of hope speak with a powerful voice as changes occur.

Change Is Not Decay

Let us quit linking together the words *change* and *decay*. Let us think of some other words instead of *decay*—such as, *better, more interesting, new, challenge, hope,* and on and on. If a change has come into your life, it is not necessarily a defeat.

Neither society nor a person can grow without change. When Jesus taught us to pray "Thy kingdom come on earth," He was saying to us to commit ourselves to bringing about changes in the world in which we live. Sometimes changes involve suffering, tragedy, and even failure, but change also can mean victory and joy and achievement. Change has the power to almost dehumanize persons, but it also has the power to enlarge us, and make us better.

In her book *Let Love Come Last,* Taylor Caldwell put it this way:

> Can you imagine how impossible the CONSTITUTION would be if we didn't continually add amendments? Amendments are signs that the Constitution is in a healthy state, and growing constantly. Whenever a man, or nation, changes its opinions, or enlarges them, he, or it, hasn't as yet died.

Hold Fast to Important Values

On the other hand, when changes come into our lives let us remember to hold fast to the important values that make life worth living. Let us remember to save the old that is worth saving. Even though many of our social customs have changed, we still maintain certain manners. It is good—I say, essential—to continue to remember to say *Please* and *Thank you*. It is a thrilling thing to walk through a great art museum and see there the works of the masters of previous generations. Even though new art forms have come in, we can continue to cherish the masterpieces of the past. The furniture that we use in our houses, for the most part, is different from what it was in past times. Yet many people continue to cherish some antique piece of furniture. It is more valuable now than when it was first created.

It is the same in our lives and in our characters. Our situations do change. Life is not the same, but there are certain human and spiritual values which we hold fast.

In the midst of change, one of the strengthening and uplifting exercises we can engage in is listing the things in our lives that we think are important enough to hold on to—no matter what happens. Holding onto these "changeless" values gives us strength when we need it the most.

17 Do Not Be Too Patient

As we think about change, it is also good to have a few thoughts about patience. In the Book of James we read, "Let patience have her perfect work . . ." (James 1:4). There are times when we do need to be patient. On the other hand, since we do live in a world of change, impatience is also an attribute to be desired and cultivated. Einstein is said to have attributed his success in his scientific studies to the fact that he "had learned to challenge an axiom." We all know that an *axiom* is a universally recognized truth, but a few people refuse to accept axioms. Just because a situation is as it is does not mean that it cannot be challenged. There are times when we need to rebel against conditions as they are. There are times when we need to be disgruntled and complaining people. Patience is a glorious asset, but patience does not necessarily mean blind acceptance.

There are times when life is changing that we do need to be patient. This patience means endurance—sticking it out—hanging on—not giving up.

Impatience as an Asset

On the other hand, impatience can be one of man's greatest assets—that is, the unwillingness to accept things as they are. I remember well when the doctor told my wife and me that our son had symptoms of polio. I could easily imagine my child being crippled for life. It was a frightening and disturbing time. Today, I do not worry about my grandchildren having polio. Somebody became so impatient with polio that he found a way to eliminate it.

A friend of mine tells about going on a camping trip with a professor from a great university, which is noted for its research. In the camp there were mosquitoes of enormous size which disturbed them greatly. The professor said, "If I could take six of my research friends from my university, and force them to live in this valley for one summer—and suffer these mosquitoes—they would find a way to get rid of them before the next summer. The trouble is, the people in this valley have been patient too long with these mosquitoes."

Amidst the difficulties of life there are always two possible views. One is the short view, which is most common. The other is the long view. In the midst of our troubles, most of us wonder what is going to happen tomorrow or next week or next month. In the short view we see only the tragedy. The long view, however, lifts our sight to the hills of time. Sometimes we say, "This is the end." We need to remember that the world has never seen "the end." I find great difficulty with the comments of some of my religious friends as they talk about "the end of the world." I have no idea when this world is coming to an end. One thing I do know is that God is never coming to an end, because God is eternal; and because of God there literally is no end for any of us. Lives change, circumstances become different. We have to readjust, but it is not the end.

Who Is Running Things?

When we come to those times that we feel like abandoning our ideals, giving up the struggle, and quitting life, it is a stimulating experience to ask ourselves some very important questions, such as: Who created this universe? Who is running things? Who determines the final outcome? Can God be defeated by evil? In view of the change that is coming to my life, is anything left for me? Am I a completely paralyzed person? Is there something I can do? Should I just fold my hands and suffer patiently?

James would certainly not have us believe that patience means sitting down and doing nothing. Patience endures today, while it works for tomorrow. Each of us has our thing—a work to do—something to stand for—some things that cannot be lost.

The more we think about it, the more we understand that *patience* and *impatience* can walk hand in hand through life, giving strength, hope, and victories.

Face the Situation

In the midst of difficult circumstances there are at least two things that we can and should do:

(1) Let's face the situation as it is. There is an old story of two men who were riding on a train through the outskirts of a large city. One of them reached over and pulled down the shade, saying, "I cannot stand to look at the sordid conditions of the slum area through which we are passing." His companion replied, "It may be there is nothing we can do at the moment about the conditions, but at least we can keep the shade up." So it is in our own lives. Just closing our eyes to the situations as they are is not going to solve any problems. Even though we do not know the answers,

we can keep looking at life's situations and recognizing their existence.

Self-distrust

(2) Next we need to develop some "self-distrust." To use the word *distrust* here seems paradoxical. But really it is very important and essential. There are times when we need to confess our own failures. There are moments when we need to believe that we are not strong enough. Oftentimes, strengthening humility comes in confessing our own failures. Sometimes our hope for tomorrow is based upon abandoning our self-confidence and self-reliance. Then it is that we look for help and support beyond ourselves.

It is true that self-distrust leads to a sense of moral and spiritual unworthiness. But this is good. Jesus told the story about two men who went to the church to pray. One of them prayed, "God, I thank Thee that I am not as other men are." The other man prayed, "God be merciful to me, a sinner." Jesus pointed out that when we exalt ourselves, then we become degraded, and when we humble ourselves we become exalted (*see* Luke 18:11–14).

The power to keep going really begins with recognizing our foibles and failures. Out of recognizing our weaknesses comes a reaching out for strengths and wisdom that is beyond ourselves. There is a story that once pianist Arthur Rubinstein was visiting in New York. His host asked him if he would like to attend church on Sunday morning. He replied, "Yes, if you will take me to hear a preacher who will challenge me to do the impossible." As we face the truth of our lives, and as we begin to believe there is a tomorrow and there is help, we take on new life, and even new, thrilling adventures.

18 Adjustments Can Be Made

As we go along through life we come to adjustments which must be made but oftentimes are difficult. One of the most serious is a physical handicap. In the church where I am the minister, the services each Sunday are on both television and radio. Recently, one of the ministers on our staff was visiting the Veteran's Hospital in this city. As the minister walked into a ward where there were several patients, one of them recognized him and spoke. He said, "I was watching the services from your church yesterday as you sang the song 'Standing on the Promises.' I lost both of my legs in the war in Viet Nam. The promises are all I can stand on."

Again and again, physical changes come into our lives which demand difficult adjustments.

Our Personal Limitations

We must also make adjustments to our personal limitations. Across the years, I have counseled with many students who had the desire to be among those in the top of the class, but simply did not have the intellectual capacity to make it. Often one becomes overwhelmed by a sense of unworthiness and shame and insecurity. It is not easy to face the fact that mentally and emotionally we are not equal to our dreams.

Defects in Those We Love

There is another adjustment that must often be made. It is adjusting to defects in those we love. As I counsel with couples who are planning marriage, one of the things I emphasize is that each must accept the other. Marriage is not a reformatory. Many divorces come out of one married partner's trying to make the other partner something he or she cannot be. There are times when divorce seems to be the only answer, but there are many marriages that could be saved, if one would learn to accept and adjust. Parents must learn this lesson in reference to children. It is a painful experience when we come to the point of realization that our little boy or girl is not the brightest and smartest in the entire world. It is even more painful, later on in life, when we realize that one of our children has imperfections that disappoint us, and even break our hearts. But we do not give up on our love. Sometimes we love "on account of" and other times we love "in spite of."

I Cannot Sing

In spite of what has happened, and in spite of what the condition is now, let us insist that an adjustment can be made. I do not mean that we simply fold our hands and endure our hardships. We need to analyze our life situation to distinguish between that part which can be changed and that part which forever must remain the same.

I personally have a deep love for the hymns of the church. I read them, I study them, and I want to sing them. I do try at times to sing, but my friends remind me that my singing is painfully inadequate. Oftentimes, I have stood at the pulpit and forgotten that the television or radio microphone was there. I would start singing with great joy. The only problem was that my voice coming through the microphone was very uninspiring. Often, I am reminded not to sing at the pulpit. I have had to adjust to the fact that I simply cannot sing.

However, once I was discussing this disappointment of mine with a very wise minister. He made this statement to me: "I have never known a preacher who could sing who was not hurt by it." I asked him to explain. His explanation was that when a preacher can sing, there is a tendency to depend on his singing instead of his preaching. He further explained that a church is more concerned about a preacher's preaching than about a preacher's singing. He said to me that because I could not sing, I had given more attention to my preaching, and that has been to my advantage. In one form or another, that is true of nearly every person. Having limitations in one area leads us to strengthen ourselves in another area. This is an adjustment to be made.

Life Remains Open-ended

As we make adjustments in life, we also need to remember that life forever remains open-ended. The last word has yet to be spoken. Handicaps can be overcome. Life can drive away the darkness. Prisons may be unlocked. The lost may be found. Meaningful existence may be discovered.

In fact, because of our faith in God, adjustment is absolutely certain. This does not mean that we simply surrender and sit down, or that some magic or supernatural power will suddenly break all the laws of nature and change everything. It does mean that God works in us and through us, leading to a solution that otherwise we would never have found.

God enters our lives much more than we realize, but often very unobtrusively. Sometimes when we are about to speak or write an indignant word, we are suddenly forced to pause and reconsider.

Sometimes we hear the laughter of a child, or song on the radio, or a sudden thought enters our mind, or we see an article in a newspaper or magazine—trivial things happen that bring lasting changes in life. The truth is, adjustments have been made every day of our lives. We just did not recognize them as they came. The minor adjustments have been made day after day after day, and when we come to that major adjustment, we have the faith to believe it, too, can be made. So be it.

As I think of adjustments, I think of those men who first followed Jesus Christ. They were not tramps or loafers. They were citizens of their country making their living. When they saw Jesus, they saw something more important than what they were doing. They were inspired to give up the life to which they had given themselves, and follow this young minister. What a tremendous adjustment they were called upon to make!

But then Jesus died, and when He died, the meaning and purpose to which they had dedicated themselves died also. There, again, a tremendous adjustment was called for. There was nothing left to do but go back and pick up their old lives as best they could.

Then, suddenly, something happened. They realized that Jesus was again in their midst, challenging them to new and greater responsibility.

As we move through life, we hear thrilling calls and see challenging opportunities. But we also experience disappointments, defeats, and sometimes life loses its meaning. Then, along the way, as we keep going, we see new paths to follow, new mountains to climb, new hopes to cling to.

Discover Life's Highest Truths

We have unmeasured power to meet disappointment and defeat as long as we believe that we can keep on going. But when the moment comes that we can see no hope, then the adjustment of going back and starting over again is well-nigh impossible. However, it is in this moment that we well may discover life's highest and most important truths.

Because of the death of Jesus, His disciples came to realize that there is another and greater dimension to life. They came upon the greatest truths that mankind could ever learn.

They were practical, sensible, hardworking people. They knew that life went by rather quickly. They had friends and loved ones who had died. Some died at a relatively early age. Some had lived to be elderly, but even so, life was short. When death came, that was the end of it. All they had left were memories. After the death of a loved one, the only thing remaining was to go back and pick up life again as best one could. So were their feelings when Jesus died. Everything about Him was gone—His power, His goodness, His love, His miracles, and certainly His presence. It is very likely that they felt cheated, and they felt they would have been better off had they never known Him at all.

Then He reappeared to them. They were gathered together on Sunday evening after He had died when, suddenly, there He was, standing in their midst, saying unto them, ". . . Peace be unto you," and further saying, ". . . as my Father hath sent me, even so send I you"

(John 20:19–21). They realized Jesus was not dead, nor was He powerless, and their lives in service to Him were not over—that they now had even greater things to live for. They realized that life has more than one dimension. Many times when we think that opportunity is dead, another and larger opportunity is being spread before us.

At this moment, let us bring to mind the experience of Franklin D. Roosevelt. Here was a man who had everything—social position, wealth, charm, ability, success in life—he seemed to have it all. Then one day he was stricken with polio. He was with his family at their summer home at Campobello. In the wonderful play *Sunrise at Campobello* by Dore Schary, we hear Mr. Roosevelt speaking to his wife these words:

> Eleanor, I must say this—once to someone. Those first few days at Campobello when this started, I had despair—deep, sick despair. It wasn't the pain—there was much more of that later on when they straightened the tendons in my legs. No, not the pain—it was the sense that perhaps I would never get up again. Like a crab lying on its back. I'd look down at my fingers, and exert every thought to get them to move. I'd send down orders to my legs and toes—they didn't obey . . . . I turned to my faith . . . for strength to endure. I feel I have to go through this fire for some reason. Eleanor, it's a hard way to learn humility—but I've been learning by crawling. I know what it meant—you must learn to crawl before you can walk.

The Accomplishments

Of course, we know that Franklin D. Roosevelt went on to achieve: the only man in the history of the United States to be elected president four times. He never became able to walk on those legs again. He had to make a tremendous adjustment, but paralyzed legs or not, he not only learned to move about, he learned to become literally the world's most powerful leader at one point in his life.

Of course, there are constant changes to be made as we go along, but those changes can be made, and we can keep going along. We don't stop; we don't give up hope.

19 Preacher, Tell Them They Can

Bishop Hazen Werner tells the story of a man who would constantly say to his pastor, "Preacher, tell them they can—tell them they can." There is a story back of that man.

Despite the background of a fine family and a good start in life, he had thrown himself away. His friends had tried long and hard to help him, until, one by one, they had given up on him. Finally, one Sunday morning, his last friend left him at the door of a rescue mission with enough tickets for two days' lodging and meals. His parting words were, "Go in there; maybe they can help you."

The first day and night he was too drunk to be helped. The second night he didn't sleep; instead, he paced the floor, and kept praying over and over, "Oh, God, if You can save a person like me, do it now. I am at the end of my rope." God did it! The man left that mission with a new spirit, a new determination, a new confidence—a new person. He is the man who said, "Preacher, tell them they can."

This is the message we need to hear when life seems hopeless. We need to know that there is still something we can do. Franklin D. Roosevelt got up from a bed of paralysis to become the leader of the world. Those first disciples of Jesus were moved from the defeat they felt when Jesus died to a feeling that they could conquer the world. The Bible refers to those disciples as ". . . These that have turned the world upside down . . ." (Acts 17:6).

In spite of what has happened, there is no doubt that every person can rise out of the ashes of defeat. The first step is *believing you can.* The greatest American psychologist who ever lived, William James, put it this way: "Our belief at the beginning of a doubtful undertaking is the one thing that insures us the successful outcome of our venture." Notice he said "the one thing." When you reach a point that you believe you can, tremendous and marvelous things can be brought to pass.

The Most Popular Bible Chapter

The most popular chapter in the entire Bible is the Twenty-third Psalm. It is beautiful and inspiring poetry, but that is not the reason it is the number-one chapter in the Bible. The reason the Twenty-third Psalm is the favorite of so many people is that it has changed their lives. It can change any life when given a chance.

It begins with the words "The Lord . . . ." Let's stop right there for a moment. There is power in the conviction that God is, and our belief begins, not with ourselves, but with God.

The psalmist goes on to describe God as "my shepherd." David, the author of this psalm, does not talk about "our" shepherd. He thinks of a God who is concerned with *him,* and we remember the words of Jesus when He said, ". . . he calleth his own sheep by name . . ." (John 10:3). God is a personal God. He knows each one of us by name. He cares for each person, one by one. He acts on behalf of each individual. And so the psalmist says, "I shall not want." He has confidence to believe that there is a resource that can meet his every need in this life.

As we read the Twenty-third Psalm, we come to those words, "Yea, though I walk through the valley of the shadow of death, I will fear no evil: for thou art with me . . . ." This refers to any difficult experience of life. Death is certainly one of those "valley" experiences. Disappointment is another. Loneliness is another. Physical illness is another. It was Henry Ward Beecher who said that the Twenty-third Psalm is the nightingale of the Psalms. The nightingale sings its sweetest when the night is the darkest. As we come to these valleys in life, it is in those experiences that many times our faith is the strongest, and God's light is the brightest. Belief in God does not guarantee the elimination of trouble from our lives. However, our faith in God does mean that no matter what happens, we can keep on going. As we read those words, let us underscore that word *through*. We walk *through* these valleys; we do not mire down in the midst of these difficult or heartbreaking experiences. We have the power to keep going.

Because of this, then, the psalmist concludes with a mighty crescendo of faith: "Surely goodness and mercy shall follow me all the days of my life . . . ." That is, "surely tomorrow will be good"—not "maybe" but "surely." In spite of whatever happens, without exception, tomorrow *can* be good. The clouds may hang dark and heavy on the horizon of one's life today, but we may be sure that the sun is shining behind those clouds, and tomorrow the sun is sure to break through. We do not need to walk the balance of our lives in the shadow.

So we can keep on insisting there is no need to "throw in the towel."

Your Greatest Obstacle

I suggest to each one reading these words, think quietly for a few moments, and consider this question, "What is the greatest obstacle in my life?" After you have decided that, then I would like for you to read the words of Jesus, which are tremendously powerful. I suppose no person can say that any one statement of the Lord is his or her favorite. Everything He said is our favorite. However, in my own life I think I have come pretty close to making the guiding principle of my life these words of Jesus:

> . . . If ye have faith as a grain of mustard seed, ye shall say unto this mountain, Remove hence to yonder place; and it shall remove; and nothing shall be impossible unto you.
>
> Matthew 17:20

There is rarely a day that ever passes that I do not quote those words. There are times, in the words of Leslie D. Weatherhead, when "my lamp flickers." I know the meaning of sorrow and disappointment, and fear and worry, and all the destructive emotions. I know there are times when faith is hard to come by, and then I read that Jesus said that if I have—not a great, big, perfect faith—if I have as much faith "as a grain of mustard seed," I can move a mountain. A grain of mustard seed is a tiny little seed. It encourages us to realize that we do not have to have a great, big, strong faith. If we just have a little bit, then, He said, we can say "unto *this* mountain . . . ." Underscore that word *this*. It is a particular mountain; it is referring to that one obstacle in your life, that one experience or difficulty, or handicap, or whatever may be blocking you. We are being told that if you will just use the little faith you have, you can move that particular mountain in your life.

In another place Jesus says that mountain can be "cast into the sea" (Mark 11:23). That means it can be buried, it can be gotten rid of, it can be forever gone. It need not haunt you the rest of your life. It can be overcome. It ceases to be an impediment in your living. It can be removed once and for all, and forever.

Then Jesus adds, ". . . Nothing shall be impossible unto you" (Matthew 17:20). When we are tempted to throw in the towel, we have a tendency to think about our troubles, instead of our triumphs—to emphasize our fears, instead of our faith—to fill our minds with our problems, instead of our powers—to concentrate on our sins, instead of our Saviour. Once we begin to exercise our faith, then we begin to think about our *possibilities*. I can think of nothing more exciting than the idea that the impossibilities of life are eliminated, and we do not have to be devastated by some defeat.

In summary, let us remember that we do not have to possess a great, big, complete faith. Rather, the faith as big as a tiny grain of mustard seed is sufficient. Second, concentrate on the one obstacle in your life. Jesus did not say that faith can move "these mountains." Rather, He said "this mountain." Get that one obstacle out of the way, and then the rest comes easier. And instead of throwing in the towel, emphasize your possibilities, remembering His words: "and nothing shall be impossible unto you."

He Leadeth Me

In "pastures green"? Not always; sometimes He
Who knoweth best, in kindness leadeth me
In weary ways, where heavy shadows be.

Out of the sunshine, warm and soft and bright,
Out of the sunshine into darkest night;
I oft would faint with sorrow and affright.

Only for this—I know He holds my hand.
So whether in the green or desert land,
I trust, although I may not understand.

And by "still waters"? No, not always so;
Oft times the heavy tempests round me blow,
And o'er my soul the waves and billows go.

But when the storms beat loudest, and I cry
Aloud for help, the Master standeth by,
And whispers to my soul, "Lo, it is I."

Above the tempest wild I hear Him say,
"Beyond this darkness lies the perfect day,
In every path of thine I lead the way."

So whether on the hill-tops high and fair
I dwell, or in the sunless valleys where
The shadows lie—what matter? He is there.

And more than this; where'ere the pathway lead
He gives to me no helpless, broken reed,
But His own hand, sufficient for my need.

So where He leads me I can safely go;
And in the blest hereafter I shall know
Why, in His wisdom, He hath led me so.

AUTHOR UNKNOWN

20 To Find Your Life—Lose It

One of the things we constantly work at in life is being responsible for ourselves. Then, when we finally almost reach that goal, we are told that we must double the load and take responsibility for somebody else. At the very beginning, we need to recognize that there are some problems that we just cannot solve. Through the years, I have spent many hours with people facing all manner of difficult situations. Some of these I have talked with have been helped. Here I would like to print a letter I received from a dear lady who came to see me in deep trouble. She later wrote to me:

> I love you. I do not mean I love you in the sense a daughter loves her father; a sister her brother; a wife her husband, nor a sweetheart her betrothed. No, I love you in a very different, special way. I now understand, in its truest meaning, our Lord's newest commandment, "LOVE ONE ANOTHER."
>
> In my entire life I have spoken with you but for one hour. Yet, this was my finest hour for I was in the presence of a Christlike divine goodness.
>
> As you sat across the desk from me, I knew, with your keen perception, you were aware of my every limitation—every weakness—every flaw—every frailty

which is a part of my being. Yet, you spoke not of imperfections; rather, gently and kindly you charted my course.

As you spoke, with deep sincerity and conviction, I came to realize Christ was not in some far-distant place; but here. I needed only to ask and He would take my hand, leading me out of the dark chasms of fear into the bright sunlight of faith.

You taught me the wonder of believing; to take the mortar of my life and build of it a cathedral of strength; to reach heavenward and touch a star.

You imbued my conscience with a desire to embody the gold of a steadfast character and to shun the tinseled sham of pretense.

You taught me where there is love, there can be no hate; where there is light, there can be no darkness; where there is good, there can be no evil.

"Be thankful," you told me, "for tribulations. One must taste sorrow to feel compassion; overcome resistance to gain achievement; and embrace humility to acquire stature and greatness."

"Look with your heart" you said, "and you will find beauty in a toilworn hand that smooths a fevered brow; a wrinkled face whose eyes light up at some small kindness, or a little child's trust."

Because you have done more for me than any creed could have done to strengthen my faith—more than any fate could have done to bring meaning and serenity into my life; I have counted it a privilege and a blessing to have touched shoulders with you.

It is then with a grateful heart, I humbly thank you, one of God's dedicated ministers, for giving me MY FINEST HOUR.

Very sincerely yours,

Of course, I cherish that letter. On the other hand, I have many times felt like some of the disciples of Jesus felt at the foot of the Mountain of Transfiguration. There a father came bringing his sick son to be healed. The father said to Jesus that he had previously spoken to His disciples, but they could not help the boy. Then Jesus performed a wonderful miracle. Later, when the disciples were alone with Jesus, they asked the question, "Why could we not do what you did?" (You will find this story in chapter 9 of Mark's Gospel.)

Again and again, I have asked myself the same question, "Why could I not help that person?"

Share the Grief

One answer is, that there are some situations that nobody can help. Some time ago I visited with a father whose teenage son had just hours before been killed in an accident. A friend was there with him, but the friend felt great despair. He said to me, "I have prayed with him; I have read him the Bible; I have tried to talk to him, but nothing helps. He will not respond to me in anyway." I sat down with him and simply said, "I do not see how you can stand to bear what has happened." The man looked up to me in a most responsive way.

Once there was a little child who went on an errand for her mother. She was late coming back and her mother asked for an explanation. The child explained that a playmate of hers down the street had fallen and broken her doll and that she had helped her. The mother wondered what she could do to help mend the broken doll. The little girl made a marvelous reply, "I just sat down and helped her cry." There are times when with other people, we cannot solve their problems, we can only become a part of their grief.

Sometimes Acceptance Is the Answer

Also, we need to know that some people are not going to change. Not every person with a drinking problem is going to stop drinking. Sometimes we just have to learn to live with it. There are teenagers in some homes that are not going to conform, and all parents can do in these cases is just the best they can to live through it, hoping that eventually the teenager will outgrow it. Over and over I have dealt with abnormal grief, and failed to help. I have watched people over a prolonged period, when their grief was devastating and self-destructive, hoping against hope that I could be patient and understand that somehow a break would come. There have been many times when the best help I could offer was not enough.

Long ago, I learned that there are situations that I just cannot handle and am compelled to accept. I heard about a man who went to a marriage counselor about his wife. He explained that she was a terrible housekeeper and he just could not stand to live in a house that was constantly in utter disorder. He had begged, pleaded, complained, and done everything he knew to get his wife to keep the house better, but nothing helped. As he talked with the marriage counselor, he was very fair to point out his wife's good qualities. Among the other things, she was beautiful, intelligent, and a very loving wife and mother. He could not understand why she wouldn't keep the house better. Finally, the wise counselor said, "Let's face it—you are married to a beautiful, intelligent, loving, lousy housekeeper!"

And in this business of helping people, let's you and I face the fact that there are some people that just are not going to be helped. They need to be accepted as they are.

Times to Leave the Results in God's Hands

However, let's go back to the story of the father who brought his sick son to Jesus. The disciples had tried to heal the boy, but had failed. However, at the close of the day, the boy was healed. In our helpless moments we need to realize that there is help beyond our abilities. There are times when we need to leave the results in God's hands.

Let People Know That You Care

Some time ago, I received an anonymous letter which contained these words. I do not know whether they were original or not. I wish I knew how to get in touch with the person who sent it. In reading this, I do know these words express the feeling of a lot of people all around us.

> I cry out in vain.
> I look and no one sees.
> I speak and no one listens.
> I think and no one understands.
> I love and no one cares.
> I exist and no one knows.
> Must I bear this insanity alone?
> The ones I care for most could care less.
> This life—must I live this hell?
> And yet life goes on.
>
> I tread where no man dares to go.
> I border on insanity.
> And the sane seem insane.

Has all the world lost all sense of direction?
I offer myself as a sacrifice—
And no one accepts the challenge.
Will those who care come forth?
And love me.

With no love I shall surely perish.
God forbid.

AUTHOR UNKNOWN

Through the years I have spent countless hours counseling with troubled people. Over and over, I have begun those counseling sessions with these words, "Tell me your situation." Most of the time, that is all a person needs, that is, somebody who will listen and let them talk about their lives. There are vast numbers of people who believe that nobody is interested in them. It does not take a wise person to do this, and my suggestion to many people who feel defeated and useless in life is that they begin taking an interest in somebody else.

Mr. Sam Rayburn was Speaker of the United States House of Representatives longer than any other man in our history. There is a story about him that reveals the kind of a man he really was.

The teenage daughter of a friend of his died suddenly one night. Early the next morning the man heard a knock on his door and when he opened it, there was Mr. Rayburn standing outside.

The Speaker said, "I just came by to see what I could do to help."

The father replied in his deep grief, "I don't think there is anything you can do, Mr. Speaker. We are making all the arrangements."

"Well," Mr. Rayburn said, "have you had your coffee this morning?"

The man replied that they had not taken time for breakfast. So Mr. Rayburn said that he could at least make coffee for them. While he was working in the kitchen, the man came in and said, "Mr. Speaker, I thought you were supposed to be having breakfast at the White House this morning."

"Well, I was," Mr. Rayburn said, "but I called the President and told him I had a friend who was in trouble, and I couldn't come."

Time and again, there are people in our lives whose problems we cannot solve, but there is *something* we can do. There is marvelous power that comes back to us when we begin doing something for somebody else.

21 Love Overcomes Fear

". . . perfect love casteth out fear . . ." said Saint John in the long ago (1 John 4:18). Modern medicine and psychology finally caught up with the Bible and confirm that truth. John is talking about the two strongest emotions of the human system—love and fear—and he says love has the power to destroy fear.

Physicians today tell us that from 50 to 75 percent of all of our sicknesses are caused by our emotions. Emotion is simply the ability to feel. Keep telling yourself that you feel sick and you will be sick. If you are sick, more than half of the time, your sickness will be cured simply by convincing yourself that you feel well.

We have physical bodies and we also have feelings or emotions. Basically all of our emotions are good, but if any of them get out of control, then they are bad. Like fire. Fire is one of the greatest benefactors of man. But uncontrolled fire can burn up a man's house and even the man himself.

Destructive Emotions

There are four main groups of destructive emotions: *fear, sense of failure, anger, pride*. Actually, even these emotions are good, as long as we can control them, but when we let them get out of hand, they make us sick in many ways.

(1) There is the *fear* group, including anxiety, worry, and apprehension.
(2) *Anger* is the father of another group of destructive emotions. Some of the children of anger are hostility, resentment, envy, jealousy, and hatred. However, anger is closely related to fear because we do not feel hostile toward a person, until we become afraid that person can hurt us in some way.
(3) A third group of destructive emotions are headed up by what we feel as a *sense of failure*. This leads to such things as discouragement, depressed moods, and various guilt feelings. Without this family of emotions there would be no repentance, but they can also lead to self-destruction.
(4) *Pride* is the captain of another army of sickening emotions, including prejudice, selfishness, self-consciousness, and conceit.

When John says, "Perfect love casteth out fear," I think that by *fear,* he has in mind all of the destructive emotions, because they are all a part of fear or stem from fear. And when he talks about *love,* he means all of the healing emotions, because love is the basis of them all.

There is *faith,* which makes us believe, and *hope,* which keeps us looking upward and forward, ". . . but the greatest of these is love" said Paul (1 Corinthians 13:13 RSV). God's Book tells us that if you have perfect love in your heart, it will drive out your fears and worries, your angers and jealousies, your failures and guilts, and make you a well, balanced, and happy person.

In other words, John says the only way to destroy our sickening emotions is developing our healing emotions.

The Fear of Failure

In Matthew 25:14–30 Jesus tells the story of a man who had three servants. Before the man left on a long journey, he gave to one of his servants five talents, to another two, and to another one. Two of the servants invested their talents in such a way as to double them.

The third servant did not use his. When the man returned, he highly complimented the two servants who did so well. He had harsh words indeed for the servant who did nothing. In explaining his failure, the servant said, "I was afraid" (v. 25).

One of our most sickening fears is that fear of failure. That fear has made invalids out of many healthy people.

We have made success one of our gods, and we fall down and worship before it. Parents are often overly ambitious for their children. Not having reached the goals in life they desired, they relive those ambitions in their children, seeking a vicarious satisfaction, as the child succeeds.

Many children have been driven into this paralyzing fear of failure. I have talked with people who were afraid to attempt even the simplest undertakings. Often you find that parents or teachers ridiculed them as children for even the smallest of failures. Many children have had this fear instilled in them by being unfavorably compared with more brilliant or capable children.

That is always the wrong approach. A person hungers for appreciation, just as he hungers for bread, and without appreciation no person can be his best. Some people think that if you compliment a person it will make him conceited. That is not true.

Look into your own heart and you will see that expressed appreciation makes you humble, never conceited. Because our hunger for appreciation is so great, if we do not receive it from others, we will bestow it upon ourselves. We will praise and magnify ourselves and self-conceit is the result. Conversely, when this basic hunger for appreciation is satisfied by others, one becomes truly humble.

A friend of mine tells of a boy who was a problem child from the time he was in the first grade. Almost every teacher he had assumed he was a hopeless case.

It was discovered the boy's parents had the cruel tendency to find fault. The boy was beaten, shouted at, and ridiculed for his mistakes. At sixteen the boy had quit school and gone to work for the manager of an amusement park.

This manager was not a trained psychologist, but he did have a kind, understanding heart. He was a man of love, and it was natural for him to praise and thank the boy for each job he did well. The boy little by little quit thinking of failure as he began receiving the one thing for which his heart had been longing.

Appreciating love cast out his fear.

Something to Live For

I have the case histories of two women who had almost identical operations.

One of the women was a shy, sensitive, overprotected person. The operation was very successful but the lady was constantly depressed. She talked constantly of "the terrible thing" which had happened to her. She talked about how she would never be able to take care of herself. Three or four weeks after the operation she died.

As far as the operation was concerned, the case of the other woman was the same. However, her operation had been postponed until her baby was born. Her operation was performed two weeks later. In two more weeks she was at home and soon she was completely recovered.

She had no time to lie around a hospital and pamper herself. She had a baby and that baby needed her. The deepest feeling she had was her love for that baby. I cannot write a definition of perfect love, but the love of a mother for her baby is the best example of perfect love that I know. Her love cast out all her fears about herself, and instead of dying, as did the first woman, she quickly was healed.

There was a girl who was brought to a hospital and died within a short time. Following the autopsy the physician said to the girl's mother, "We could find no cause of death." The mother replied, "Oh, doctor, you don't have to tell me why she died. She died of a broken heart. The young man to whom she was engaged was killed a few weeks ago. Since that time she has had no interest in anything."

Of a broken heart. That means she had lost her love. Very often the loss of love means the loss of security, maybe the loss of self-respect. Frequently when love is crushed, one becomes overwhelmed with the feeling of being not needed or not wanted. That can be and often is, fatal. It can destroy in a person any desire to live and consciously or subconsciously that person begins to desire death. The desire for death becomes stronger than the instinct for self-preservation. Thus one *does* die of a broken heart.

The cure. Jesus said, ". . . he that loseth his life for my sake shall find it" (Matthew 10:39); or again, "Seek ye first the kingdom of God, and his righteousness; and all these things shall be added unto you" (Matthew 6:33).

That is, when you give yourself to something greater than yourself, when some great cause becomes more important than your own life, and to that cause you give all of your interests and feelings, then that cause will give back to you a stronger and healthier life than you ever experienced before.

Self-centeredness makes us sick. Perfect love heals us.

We Gain by Giving

Abraham Lincoln and his law partner, William Herndon, were arguing the question of whether or not any person ever performs a completely unselfish act. They were riding together through the country and came upon a pig caught in a rail fence. Herndon pretended not to see the animal.

But Lincoln stopped, got down and waded through a muddy ditch, pulled the rails apart and released the pig. Herndon pointed triumphantly to Lincoln's muddy shoes and spattered trousers, saying, "You see now I am right. Men are capable of performing unselfish deeds."

"Oh, no," replied Lincoln, "if I had left that pig in the fence, I would have worried about him all night. I would have been so busy wondering if someone had rescued him, or if he was still held between those rails that I would have lost my sleep. For my own peace of mind, I had to rescue the animal. So you see, I was merely being selfish."

Without entering the argument of Lincoln and Herndon as to whether or not a person is capable of performing a completely unselfish act, that story does illustrate the fact that failure to give may sometimes be very costly. In Lincoln's case, it would have cost him a night's sleep and his peace of mind.

"For God so loved the world that he gave . . . ." Love is a process of giving. In fact, love demands expression and if it is not expressed, it becomes a poison for one's own soul.

In order to have love come into our lives, first we must express our love for others. "The song is to the singer, and comes back most to him; The gift is to the giver, and comes back most to him; The love is to the lover, and comes back most to him."

". . . with what measure ye mete, it shall be measured unto you . . ." said Jesus (Mark 4:24). Again He said, "Give, and it shall be given unto you . . ." (Luke 6:38).

Perfect love casteth out fear. What is the basis of fear? I think it is the possibility of losing—losing health, security, friends, or any of many things. If you have nothing to lose, then you have nothing to fear.

Perfect love gives without thought of return. Therefore, love has nothing to lose. Love has already given all that it has. Thus, love has nothing to fear. Love *does* cast out fear.

22 Here Is the Way It Works
(*A Summary of Defeat and How We React*)

To draw a picture of the average life is not difficult. We begin early in life, looking forward to what we want to do, accomplish, possess, the position we seek, the material things we are after, and the pattern of life that we want. As we grow older, this picture expands and grows. For example, when I started in my ministry, one of my greatest desires was to preach over the radio. Eventually, I got that opportunity and have been regularly on radio for thirty-five years. But, in my early ministry, television was something I did not even dream of. However, as far as I can ascertain, I had the first church service ever televised in the United States, and have been on television now for thirty years. I mention that to say that our dreams expand and many times we acquire and achieve more than we first thought possible.

There is great danger here, however, and in nearly every life that danger is realized. That is, those things we prize can be lost. A wife or a husband can die, an investment can take away material possessions. Opportunities which meant so much to us can be lost. That promotion we expected can be given to somebody else. Our lives can be so shaken that we can be literally possessed with despair. We can feel defeated, destroyed, and completely disheartened. The result can be deep sorrow.

In our society today, we are seeing an increasing amount of change. The act of moving from one city to another can for many people be traumatic. I was talking recently to a young engineer in a large corporation. At ten o'clock on Monday morning the vice-president of his company said to him, "We want you to move to another city." He asked when they expected him to report in the other city and the reply was, "We want you to be in your office there tomorrow morning at eight o'clock." He told me that he went home, packed his bag, and caught the plane that afternoon. Later his wife and children moved, but it meant taking them out of school, away from their neighborhood friends, and it meant an entire new start for the family. Uprooted families many times have great problems.

Life can be changed in many other ways. A mate can die; a divorce is granted; we can lose a job; or be retired with nothing to do. Physical disabilities can suddenly come upon us. In countless ways lives are upset.

Many times we look upon these upsetting experiences as defeats. Through these years, I have now dealt with enough men and women that I have come to believe that in some degree people's reactions to defeat follow the same pattern. On the shelves of my study are a dozen or more books dealing with the problems of life and the reactions of people. Nearly all of the authors pretty much agree. So, this summary comes not only from my own observations, but also from the observations of many colleagues in the ministry and in counseling, and dealing with people in other areas.

At First, We Do Not Feel It

Some time ago, I went to the hospital to see a young man whose leg had been broken in an accident. I asked him how it felt at the moment his leg was broken. He replied that he felt almost no pain at all. This is true of some of the "breaking" experiences of life. At the moment of some very shocking experience, it is almost as though we have been given an anesthesia. One rarely sees deep expression of grief at the moment of the death of a loved one. The grief comes later—sometimes much later. I have known people to begin reacting to some shocking experience as much as a year after it happened.

So the first stage of defeat for many people is simply not realizing that it has actually happened.

We Do Feel

Second, sooner or later, we give expression to our feelings. But people are different. Some shed bitter tears; some are very quiet and serene. One of the mistakes that parents of young children make is to say to them, "Don't cry." The ability to cry needs to be learned, just like many other abilities. It ought not to be thwarted or blanketed. A child that is not permitted to cry oftentimes is not able to cry as an adult. Crying many times is the best release that a person can have. It certainly is preferable to a so-called nervous breakdown, or even worse, to deep resentments, self-pity, or even the inability to keep on living, which may result in suicide.

The person who tries to live without expressing emotion is making a very serious mistake. We express emotion in different ways. Such expression should be one of our reactions to some unhappy circumstance. To cry is not to be devastated. In fact, crying can be a protection *against* being devastated.

We Begin to Lose Faith

Sooner or later, the normal person wonders why God allowed this or that to happen. If we decide that it happened because God did allow it, then we begin to wonder why. Many times we decide that God does not love us, and that He is not concerned about us. Questions about God come in the normal process of living, and even rejections of God are not uncommon. Then it naturally follows that we begin to wonder if we can trust other people, even our closest friend. It begins to be difficult for us to relate to other people. We fail to see that the fault is in us, and we begin blaming them. We decide that no one can be trusted, or cares, or is loving. We become very lonely, which leads to depression.

There is hardly one among us who has not at some time said with the psalmist, "Why art thou cast down, O my soul? and why art thou disquieted in me?" (Psalms 42:5). The psalmist goes on to say, ". . . hope thou in God." For the moment we have decided that God has rejected us, and during that moment, we find hope a meaningless experience. Thus our deep experience of desertion and depression. It is not bad to sometimes be unhappy. If the sun were to shine all the time, the entire world would be a desert, and sometimes we even enjoy moments of sorrow and depression and unhappiness.

We Imagine Sickness

I have a very close friend who was carried to the hospital with a heart attack. He spent the normal amount of time in the intensive care unit and went through the treatment process that is usually given to heart patients. However, six months later, one of the greatest heart specialists in America (who had been treating him) said to him that he never had any kind of heart attack at all. What he had had was a reaction to a life situation. Today, the most prescribed drug in the United States is Valium, and in addition to Valium, there are other similar drugs which are dispensed. We are living in the most affluent society the world has ever known. We are better off than any people have ever been, and yet we are taking more tranquilizers, going to more psychiatrists, and having more mental problems. Much of the illness in life today is psychosomatic. Our patterns of life change, and getting sick is one of the normal reactions.

It is extremely important to have physical checkups on a regular basis by competent physicians, and it is also extremely important to accept the verdict of the physician. If we are not sick, let's get up and get going. Instead of looking for some new medicine, let's begin looking for some new meanings in life. Here is a place where our basic beliefs about living, of our own personalities, about our own circumstances, may need to be examined. Here is a place where oftentimes maturity is what we need instead of medicine.

Panic May Be Worse Than the Pain

Some time ago, I read about a theater which was crowded with people when a fire broke out. Actually, the fire was rather quickly controlled and did very little damage. But the people became panic-stricken and many were hurt, and some even killed, as a result of their panic to escape the fire.

The same thing happens in an individual's life. Many times the panic is much worse than the experience. We are grateful today for the great progress being made in the treatment of cancer. Larger numbers of people today are being healed, but many people, when they learn they have some form of cancer, become literally panic-stricken. The same can be true of many other crisis situations.

I have often thought of my own dear mother. She was sixty years old when my father died. He was a minister and lived in a home which belonged to the church. My mother had no place to go and very little money to live on. It would have been so easy for her to have become panic-stricken, but she was a very capable and sensible person. She reasoned that somehow things would work out, and they did work out. She lived twenty-seven years after my father died, and during those years she had experiences that she never dreamed would ever come to her. For example, right after World War II, she went to Europe on a freighter and spent three weeks crossing the Atlantic. She enjoyed it thoroughly.

Many times, when one's life partner dies, the panic becomes a very serious state of mind. Usually to every problem there is a solution. When the fire breaks out in the theater, if the people would just quietly go to the exits, there is time enough for everybody to be saved. Likewise in life, there are exits from these interrupting circumstances through which we can go out into a larger life. Instead of getting panicky, we need to be open to new experiences and different relationships. Panic is normal and to be expected. But it must not be a controlling factor in our lives very long. Then it becomes destructive. So, expect the panic, but also know that it can be overcome.

"If I Had . . ."

I was riding with a dear friend of mine in a certain section of the city where I live. He pointed out some land to me and said that he considered buying that property some twenty years ago. He even went so far as to arrange the financing with his bank, but he decided against it. Now, he was telling me that that property was worth thirty times more than he could have bought it for twenty years earlier. He talked about how much money he would have today, if he had gone on and made the transaction. Then with a smile, he turned to me and said, "Long ago I learned you cannot play that 'if I had' game." All of us can look back and say, "If I had done this, or if I had done that . . . ."

We think of our children and wish we had done this or that. The same can be said of our marriage, or of our job, or most all of our life experiences.

I am thinking now of a lady about forty years old who is having extreme mental and emotional problems. Her mother died about two years ago, and ever since she has been worrying about some things she said to her mother back in other years. We can all look back on experiences with regrets. That is not so bad, but the bad part comes when those regrets become abnormal guilts. There is normal guilt and there is abnormal guilt. Normal guilt is something we face, do what we can about it, and go on. Abnormal guilt takes possession of us and has the power to literally destroy us.

It is probably true that as most people come toward the latter part of life, the one thing they would rather have than anything else, is the forgiveness of the mistakes they have made and the sins they have committed. Sooner or later, every one of us can say as David said, "Have mercy upon me, O God . . ." (Psalms 51:1). Let us be thankful that

God *is* a God of mercy. Let us also be thankful that most people are people of mercy. Normally, parents do not remember against their children things that the children said or did. Most friends do not hold grudges forever. Most of our sins and mistakes have already been forgiven. The hardest forgiveness to accomplish is our own forgiveness. Neurotic guilt becomes a very destructive emotion. Guilts that are not settled can cause misery for years to come. Let us remember that we all are guilty and somehow there comes a time when that guilt needs to be settled. If we can do something about it, in the name of heaven, let's do it. If nothing can be done about it, dismiss it and go on. You will never forget it, but you can forgive it.

Resentment Instead of Gratitude

I know a young lady who was in an automobile wreck. She was thrown into the windshield, and the glass cut her face severely. When I first saw her in the hospital, she was so thankful and grateful that her life had been spared. The wreck was very serious, and it was a miracle that she had not been killed. She expressed gratitude to God for her life and felt that because God had spared her life, she wanted to live for others as she had never done before.

However, later on she would look at those scars on her face. The surgeons did a good job in minimizing the scars, but still they were there and she felt disfigured. Actually, the disfigurement was not nearly as severe as it grew to be in her mind. That is true many times of our problems. They have a way of growing out of proportion, as we continue to think of them. Gradually, she emphasized less and less her gratitude to God for being saved, and more and more the resentment she had over those scars on her face.

Resentment is an emotion that at times all people feel, but resentment is almost always a destructive emotion. It is to be expected, but not to be nursed and cultivated and allowed to grow. I know men who, by some quirk of fate, never got the break in life that some other man got. Such a person looks at the one who prospered and realizes that he has as much ability as that man has, and gradually feels, "I live in this house and he lives in that house and it's not fair. My house should be as good as his house; my position in the community should be as high as his is; I should have as much money as he has." Resentment can become poison. Hostilities can grow to the point that we believe that life is unfair, and that God does not love us. However, it helps us to remember that this is also a normal reaction and emotion to some of life's disturbing experiences. Also, we must remember that hostilities can and must be handled. We need to assure ourselves that resentments can be overcome.

Life Must Go On

In this brief outline of a life process, let me use a personal illustration. My own dear wife was sick in the hospital for three years. She had a heart arrest with some brain damage. However, she was improving. She had made more progress the third year than she had the first two years. She was never in a coma, and I always felt that she knew me. Most of the time when I came into the room, she would begin to breathe heavier. During the three years she was in the hospital, frequently we took her downstairs in a rolling chair and she would sit on the porch and watch the cars go by, or the people who came into view. One of the things she enjoyed the most was looking at the sky. When one is constantly in a room, to go out under the sky is an exhilarating experience. Just two weeks before she died, I took her out in the yard of the hospital, and for two hours we sat together under some trees, and she was fascinated watching a flock of birds. I was so hopeful about her possibilities. I really believed that she would get well. However, she developed an infection which she could not overcome, and she died. We had her funeral in the church where I am the minister on Wednesday. Even during the service, I sat in the pew wondering how I would feel the next time I stood in that pulpit. However, I knew that I had to go back. Many of my friends suggested that I ought to take a couple of weeks off, but I felt that the quicker I went back, the better off I would be. So the next Sunday, I preached in that pulpit.

I tell my own experience to say that when life's upsetting experiences come, there is a tendency to wonder if we can start over again. The truth is that we *must* start again and we *must* keep going. Also, the quicker we get started, the easier and better it is for us. After some life-defeating experience, the longer our inactive period is, the worse off we are. Some useful activity is the best medicine for a defeated soul that can be found on this earth. We recall that when a woman's husband died, for a period of time she would observe what was called "mourning." She would wear black dresses and would pretty much withdraw from life. Our society today has learned better than that, and that so-called period of mourning has just about been eliminated. Of course, we feel sorrow, but sorrow does not mean that we have to withdraw. Sorrow does not call for inaction.

We must learn to remind ourselves that the past is past. In our memories we not only enjoy many things, but we also suffer much. We remember thoughts and words and deeds that we wish we had never had. We remember failures and defeats with sorrow and disappointment. Let us also remember that once Jesus said to a man, "Ye must be born again." One of the things that that statement means is, that we do not need to live in the past. We can also live in the future. As we think about it, surely the future is much more exciting than the past. Inactivity is one of the temptations of a life-upsetting experience. There are times when we need to "be still." I have frequently said to people who have undergone some difficult experience, "Get away alone and be quiet and think." One of the most creative experiences in life is silence, but it is something that must not be overdone. I cannot think of any worse punishment than being in solitary confinement, yet that is exactly the punishment that many people inflict upon themselves.

Psychologists and psychiatrists will tell us very positively that people need to talk about their experiences. Many times our friends are hesitant to mention this sorrow or hurt or disappointment which you face. If they do not mention it, bring it up yourself. Talking about it oftentimes is effective therapy. Withdrawal holds the poison imprisoned within us.

"Through the Valley"

Now we come to the next stage in the grief process. The psalmist said it best, "Yea, though I walk through the valley . . ." (Psalms 23:4). It really does not matter which valley we are walking through. The word to underscore is that word *through*. As we keep going, we can say with the psalmist, "I will fear no evil." The cure for fear is walking. The breeding place for fear is inactivity. As we walk through our own valley, gradually we begin to develop hope. We begin to feel that there is a solution, that this is not the end of our world, that doom does not have to be our constant possession.

In the normal course of my work, I fly a great deal. Many times I have been in an airplane that has taken off from the runway into a cloudy, threatening sky. It is not a comfortable feeling to fly into air where you cannot see, wondering if there are storms in your pathway ahead. The pilot keeps the nose of the plane upward, and then comes that wonderful moment when you break through the clouds into the sunshine.

So can it be in life. The clouds are frequently there. There is the fear of worse experiences, but we keep going and break into a new life that is bright and beautiful, and with more possibilities than we ever dared dream existed.

The World Is Still There

The triumphant moment in life's grief process is when we realize that the world is still real and we face the reality of our own lives. So many times we feel that this earthquake in our hearts has been an earthquake in the entire world, and that everything is shaken and destroyed. Then we begin to realize that our world is still there. Maybe we have lost something, but we still have most of what we did have. We begin to realize that God is still God, that people are still people, that we still have feelings, and though we have been shaken, the reality of life has not been destroyed.

As we begin to realize that really life has not changed, we do become whole again. It is not right for any person to live forever under a burden that should have been left behind and settled. We need to know that we can live—we can love—we can believe—we can hope—we can work—we can live again—we can have perfect peace.

This is a complete list of books by Charles L. Allen since he became a Revell author in 1951.

GOD'S PSYCHIATRY
THE TOUCH OF THE MASTER'S HAND
ALL THINGS ARE POSSIBLE THROUGH PRAYER
WHEN YOU LOSE A LOVED ONE
WHEN THE HEART IS HUNGRY
THE TWENTY-THIRD PSALM
THE TEN COMMANDMENTS
THE LORD'S PRAYER
THE BEATITUDES
TWELVE WAYS TO SOLVE YOUR PROBLEMS
HEALING WORDS
THE LIFE OF CHRIST
PRAYER CHANGES THINGS
THE SERMON ON THE MOUNT
LIFE MORE ABUNDANT
THE CHARLES L. ALLEN TREASURY (Charles L. Wallis)
ROADS TO RADIANT LIVING
RICHES OF PRAYER
IN QUEST OF GOD'S POWER
WHEN YOU GRADUATE (with Mouzon Biggs)
THE MIRACLE OF LOVE
THE MIRACLE OF HOPE
THE MIRACLE OF THE HOLY SPIRIT
CHRISTMAS IN OUR HEARTS (with Charles L. Wallis)
CANDLE, STAR AND CHRISTMAS TREE
(with Charles L. Wallis)
WHEN CHRISTMAS CAME TO BETHLEHEM
(with Charles L. Wallis)
CHRISTMAS (with Charles L. Wallis)
WHAT I HAVE LIVED BY
YOU ARE NEVER ALONE
PERFECT PEACE
HOW TO INCREASE SUNDAY SCHOOL ATTENDANCE
(with Mildred Parker, to be published in 1980)